THE NEW LOVE DEAL

What You *Must* Know Before Marrying, Moving In, or Moving On!

GEMMA ALLEN: View from the Bar

Judge Michele Lowrance: View from the Bench

TERRY SAVAGE: View from the Bottom Line

ISBN: 0615948081
ISBN 13: 9780615948089

Library of Congress Control Number: 2014900499
The New Love Deal, Inc.
Chicago, IL

THE NEW
LOVE DEAL

TABLE OF CONTENTS

INTRODUCTION

We know one thing about love and relationships today—something that is really difficult to admit: despite our hopes and dreams, the odds of making a relationship work are, at best, fifty-fifty. So we—a divorce attorney, a former divorce court judge turned domestic relations mediator, and a financial advisor—wrote this book to help your chances of being in the half of committed relationships that last as long as your dreams.

Our myths about permanency, consistency, and security in relationships have been assaulted in the movies, in the media, and in real life. We may all long for the good old days when marriage and relationships seemed more sustainable, but closing your eyes to reality won't make it happen. If you are reading these opening lines, we are sure you are saying to yourself: "I'm in love and I don't want to hear this!"

It's part of our DNA to want relationship security, so we recoil when the possibility is questioned. The notion of a prenuptial agreement or a relationship contract feels like an attack on your treasured survival mating master plan. We know that. So in response to this thorny dilemma, the three of us got together to figure out a way for couples to adapt to these harsher realities without destroying the romance.

We know that's what you want—a forever relationship that rises above the seemingly mundane issues of money, and property, and financial planning. You want the moonlight and flowers and the emotional high. But with an agreement or not, reality will soon set in. We believe that creating the appropriate agreement will not destroy your romance, but enhance it, because you are no longer fearful of the unspoken issues that might eventually divide you.

Perhaps, you're feeling pressure not only from each other, but from friends, parents, or an ex-spouse or adult children. They feel they should have some influence on your new relationship, whether because they have a financial stake in how you move forward, or just because they think they see potential roadblocks to your happiness.

While written relationship agreements are not new, we offer not only a different way of looking at them, but techniques to make your relationship even stronger and more sustainable. We are giving you skills and strategies for protecting your relationship, so that inevitable disagreements do not lead to avoidable breakups.

We know that it's difficult to create permanency in an era of accelerating change. You can't play the new game using the old rules of relationships. We are not living in our parents' relationship. Many people reading this book are children of divorced families, or may be helping rear children of a loved one's previous marriage or relationship.

Previous generations married for love and rarely just lived together. They trusted in the concept of "till death do us part"—whether or not they actually stayed married. Having a child out of wedlock was a public sin. Even conception before marriage was frowned upon, as family and friends counted backward nine months to the marriage date.

The world of relationships has changed dramatically, yet we have not changed our laws, our rules, or our expectations. We still believe in love and the possibility of a permanent soul mate—no matter what form these relationships take. But we need new ground rules for the many arrangements we choose to display our love. In short, we have not prepared ourselves for the New Love Deal.

The rules and roles of the Love Deal have completely changed. We are cohabiting in record numbers and marrying later. This is not just a generational issue. Census figures show that the number of cohabiting unmarried couples with at least one partner over age fifty has grown to more than 1.5 million households. That is a 500 percent increase since the mid-1990s.

For the first time in American history, more children are born out of wedlock than into traditional families. And, despite the economy forcing people to stay together for financial reasons, the divorce rate is still nearly 50 percent.

Married or not, couples are usually both employed, and incomes are likely to be uneven. These couples—married or not—buy property together, have children, and share debt. They may be same-sex couples and may have biological or adopted children.

But while we recognize these changes in social acceptability, we lack legal guidelines and procedures for navigating these turbulent waters. As a result, breakups are messy—and not only from an emotional standpoint. They are also wreaking havoc on each party's financial future—destroying credit reports, devastating retirement security, generating legal fees, and creating one financial crisis after another.

This book is about acknowledging those changes and structuring your own New Love Deal—a guideline for making your relationship succeed, or for dissolving it in a way that prevents additional tears and pain. As you read this book, you will see that we have integrated the power of love with the power of rationality to create the best outcomes for your entire life.

PLAYING THE ODDS

Fairly consistently, about two million Americans marry each year—and one million Americans divorce on that same annual basis. Truly, this is a triumph of hope over experience.

The actual marriage rate has been slipping, and more than half of young people today will at some time live with a romantic partner, whether or not they marry.

Cohabitation has commitments, obligations, and a failure rate of its own. A recent study on cohabitation by the *Boston Herald* concluded that after five to seven years, only 21 percent of these couples were still living together.

It's not our purpose to explain why these relationships fail. But we do submit that a big factor in both the breakups and the emotional pain that follows is the lack of communication about expectations—ranging from money to children to in-laws, to the simplest expectations about living arrangements. These are all the things we tend to ignore when passion burns brightly.

A big factor in both the breakups and the emotional pain that follows is the lack of communication about expectations

Very simply, while everyone may be doing the "love deed," no one is defining the New Love *Deal*.

DOING THE DEAL

The New Love Deal recognizes that any committed relationship has aspects of a business deal. Yes, a business deal. You may think it's not romantic, but we intend to challenge that notion. In fact, the very act of negotiating such an agreement bodes well for your future. It means not only that you acknowledge the potential for failure, as predicted by statistics, but that you are willing to do everything possible to ensure success.

The best relationship "deal memos" define the obligations of each party while the partnership is working—and the rights of each party if it fails. The terms should be written down and modified, if necessary, by agreement. Whether you are cohabiting, marrying, or already married but negotiating through a rough patch, the act of discussing not only financial but structural issues (who gets what, who does what, who owes what) will lead you to a better understanding of each other.

It often takes the services of an impartial mediator or legal counsel to come to this understanding, although you should work out the details together first. It is best to set up the terms of your New Love Deal before you make a commitment, or at least before you let the expensive lawyers take over during a split, and give up your power and fate to the court system.

Money is often cited as the leading cause of breakups, but we believe it is not just about the money. It's really about all the things we do not discuss before making a commitment—goals, expectations, lifestyle, conflict resolution—and communication, communication, communication. Talking about what really matters to you is not a sign of selfishness—it is a sign of trust. Writing down those things

We believe it is not just about the money.

you are willing to do and hope to accomplish is not limiting—it is the essence of a commitment.

WHO WE ARE

We are three professional women who have seen it all when it comes to money and relationships.

Gemma Allen is a prominent Chicago divorce attorney who litigates the dissolution of the relationships of those who have never addressed the dollars and "sense-and-sensibility" issues. She is a contributor to legal journals on the subject of matrimonial law, and a frequent television guest expert on relationship issues.

Michele Lowrance is a longtime divorce court judge and author of *The Good Karma Divorce*. She has been featured in a television series on couples' mediation. As a judge, she presided over thousands of marital breakups. Now, as a professional domestic relations mediator, she works with divorcing couples—and those creating prenuptial agreements.

Terry Savage is a nationally syndicated financial columnist, and the author of *The Savage Truth on Money, The Savage Number,* and several other best-selling financial planning books. She is often on CNN and other national television and radio programs, commenting on the markets and the economy and advising people on how to make smart money decisions that will provide long-term financial security.

Together, we promise to help you create the most positive, optimistic, and realistic New Love Deal—one that will go a long way to ensuring the success of your relationship dreams and will remove at least part of the heartbreak of failure, should your relationship fall apart. This won't require a lot of effort—just a willingness to look at reality and act in a way that is beneficial to both you and your partner.

Here's a closer look at who we are and our perspectives on the issues of relationships and money.

Divorce Attorney Gemma B. Allen: View from the Bar

Marriage is good for your health, good for your heart, good for children, and it can be great for wealth building. Yet, fear of a marriage ending makes many people avoid what might be the best time of their lives. Still, divorce is an emotional and economic disaster for most families. Even at its best, it is always about division.

That's where I come in. I'm a divorce attorney, so I take your side in this deal. But from long experience, I see both sides. And here's what I see: most of us have very real fears about the emotional and financial consequences of a marriage or relationship ending. As a result, we avoid thinking about the possibility. That causes huge—and expensive—problems when relationships don't work out. Instead of avoiding them, we should face our fears and commit to creating better beginnings with written agreements.

I have been both married and divorced, so I have some personal experience of the trauma involved. The most significant aspect of my background, however, is my day-to-day experience for over twenty-five years as a divorce attorney.

I started out as a lobbyist and a litigator. I only focused on family law when my mother's best friend needed a divorce attorney and insisted it be me. Since then, I have negotiated and litigated more than two thousand divorces, numerous prenuptial agreements, and even a few postnuptial agreements.

From both my personal and professional experience, I have observed these truths:

We do more planning for our weddings than we do for our marriages. It is easier to discuss sex than money, but money is just as likely to drive a couple apart—some say more likely. Not every divorce "had to be," and even the inevitable ones did not have to be so financially and emotionally draining.

We do more planning for our weddings than we do for our marriages.

Cohabitation without documentation is not the simple solution that lovers think it will be. Civil unions and domestic partnerships provide some financial and legal protection, but it is still not enough, and these arrangements can be fraught with peril when or if you move from state to state.

Above all, my profession has taught me that, whatever the relationship, if partners would treat it as a deal—the New Love Deal—when they start out, the finish would not be so brutal and expensive because couples would know in advance where they stand.

The Old-Style Prenuptials

I have always viewed the old-style prenuptial agreements with a jaundiced eye because, to be perfectly blunt, their historic goal has been for the partner with money to share as little of it as possible with his or her mate, both on death and divorce.

And traditionally, the "have-not"—usually a younger woman marrying an older or wealthier man—had little to bargain with except the obvious youth and beauty. She had to assess how much economic "fairness" she could extract before the man or his family would declare the wedding was off.

I particularly remember one beautiful young woman, whom I will call Cindy. Cindy was marrying an older multimillionaire frog—though he was a prince in her eyes. The deal for her was no deal at all—either on his death or their divorce, she would get a maximum of $100,000, assuming they had been married at least five years. While that seemed like a princely sum, at $20,000 per year it was a truly unbalanced and unfair agreement.

When she was advised not to sign, her wishful answer to the legal advice was, "He will take care of me later." The reality was that the financial arrangements did not get better and the unbalanced marriage did not last. In her case, as in the greatest majority of cases, the law upheld the contract, and she had to live with the consequences.

The New Love Deal

That old-style unfairness motivated us to empower a new generation of couples, whether they are married or just living together, to use agreements constructively. We want to help design agreements with as much attention to detail as one would pay to any other serious partnership investment. And for couples who are just planning to live together, we want to show you how to create a cohabitation agreement that will help you build your life together in the most logical and legal way.

Many women now have successful careers and/or assets of their own—and may marry or live with men who earn less or have less. Many men now acknowledge the still-existing economic inequality for women, especially for those who stop or interrupt their careers to have and nurture children. Most everyone has lived through or witnessed a devastating divorce and knows that not every marriage is made in heaven.

There are also many more couples who do not want some judge or lawyer to determine their economic future, if somehow they do not stay together. But if these couples face their issues together, the agreements they work out can be about fair sharing and not economic shaming. If marriage is a contract or if cohabitation is the agreement we have made, let's spell out the terms and bargain in good faith and in love.

BLIND JUSTICE

There are a thousand unflattering sayings about the law and lawyers. I am not sure if Shakespeare started it in *Henry VI* with his "First kill all the lawyers" line, but the trend continues. What I see every day in the courtroom is neither bad lawyers nor heartless judges—just a well-intentioned legal system trying to cope with the innumerable sorrows and financial shortfalls of marriages under siege.

There is simply no way even the best judge or lawyer can understand and balance the particular needs and unique resources of your relationship. The purpose of creating a prenuptial or cohabitation agreement is to control the law and make it serve your needs, even if separation comes along. We are all looking for a soft landing, and with our approach to the New Love Deal, you can give each other that gift.

Irreconcilable differences is one of the most common grounds for divorce. How could these differences possibly arise in spite of your loving hopes for a happy marriage? No one expects to have them, no one wants them, but half of all couples do—sooner or later. These differences can be as complex as the DNA of the two people who marry or as simple as their unspoken expectations. They are differences we cannot reconcile, or they are differences we never faced and addressed until they became bigger than our love.

If you fear finding yourself in this position, this book can help you find the answers. And for those of you choosing to just live together, we want to help you protect your assets, rights, and credit if somehow it does not work out. In most states, the law almost ignores legal complaints of an ousted cohabiter. Unless there is a written agreement as to which assets are whose and legal titles reflecting that agreement, a cohabiter can literally wind up out in the cold after a breakup.

As an attorney, I'd rather help you create your New Love Deal than guide you through the lengthy and painful litigation of a breakup with no rules except those dictated by blind justice.

JUDGE MICHELE LOWRANCE: VIEW FROM THE BENCH

I have been a family court judge for nineteen years and a divorce attorney for two decades prior, until recently becoming a certified mediator. I have witnessed too many vows that proclaimed "till death do us part" eventually coming to mean "till change do us part." Sadly, the national wedding bouquet is now composed of short-blooming daylilies. And yet, we are compelled to hold on to the concept of eternal love.

Looking deeply into our beliefs about the permanency of relationships is very painful. If we are not pushed to consider the possibilities and even the benefits of a prenuptial or cohabitation agreement, or a civil union, we probably will try to avoid it.

Illusions of a perfect union—or even semi-perfection—are the necessary component that inspires our leap of faith, driving us to the altar even in a time when we know that the divorce rate is ominously high.

The fear of a prenuptial agreement is legendary, no matter how mature we think we are. A friend confided to me: "I waited forty years to find the one woman who is perfect for me. Money comes and money goes, but love—I mean, true love—is almost impossible to find. Now that I have, and I am one of the few who have, I am afraid to blow it by asking for a prenuptial agreement."

The fear of a prenuptial agreement is legendary, no matter how mature we think we are

The friend who made that statement knew that the divorce rate for first marriages is about 50 percent. He is not the only one to hold on to the persistent belief that he or she will be out of the reach of the tentacles of those statistics. Many of us correctly believe that our connection with our partner is as unique as our fingerprints. Prince Charming searched the countryside for the one woman whose foot would fit the glass slipper. And when he finally found her, he did not pull out a document asking her to waive her rights to the kingdom!

ILLUSION VERSUS REALITY

The illusion of the invincibility of love and marriage, and now civil unions, serves a necessary function in our steel-plated world of technology, in which sentimentality may be delivered only in text messages. This belief in the concept of "happily ever after" offers one of the few soft spots remaining in our society and carries with it much pleasure.

This sacred pleasure is not just driven by romance, but by our biology. We are all hooked, or want to be hooked, on the endorphins that come with the idea of love forever and ever. Our limbic system is the cradle of wishful thinking and the birthplace of hoping to win the lottery, praying that our horse wins at the track, or believing that "this marriage will last forever." It's the part of our brain that optimistically tells us all things are possible.

I am truly sorry to spoil all those good feelings with the reality of the statistics, which I see in court every day as parties divorce and find themselves in the ultimate tug-of-war. What started out as planning by the light of the silvery moon shining gently on gold-tipped place cards next to fine china has turned into armed conflict. Yet, in the glow of romance, when you wanted to be emotionally naked with your partner, you couldn't face the idea of suiting up with the armor of protection afforded by a prenuptial agreement.

In this confusing tug-of-war, the Holy Grail of all questions is: Do cohabitation, civil union, or premarital contracts destroy our concept of fate, romance, and finding our destiny? This is followed by the related question: Can you trust completely and have an unfettered connection to your partner at the same time as the lawyer's calculator is clicking in the background?

Day in and day out, I have seen the painful drama of breakup and divorce play out as a horror movie, where couples attempt to be vindicated by convincing me that their mate is to blame and I should find the other one guilty, despite the fact that no-fault divorce means that no one is guilty.

In this confusing tug-of-war, the holy grail of all questions is: do cohabitation, civil union, or premarital contracts destroy our concept of fate, romance, and finding our destiny?

FIGHTING FAIR

Yes, I do have an agenda; I want to keep people out of court—divorce, paternity, and probate court. As a culture, we have come to love extreme fighting, in the ring as well as in court. We turn to anger as the emotion of choice, with revenge riding shotgun into the courtroom. An eye for an eye in divorce court leaves both parties blinded.

Yet many of us still consider the cohabitation, civil union, and prenuptial agreements as the cod liver oil of cohabiting or marital life. It may be good for us, but it leaves us with a bitter taste. This harsh view of protective agreements puts creative solutions into the deep freeze.

For those of you who are freethinkers, wouldn't you like to be the one to make all the decisions about your relationship or marriage?

Why let the state in which you live determine your lifestyle in the event your relationship or marriage terminates? Cohabitation, civil union, or prenuptial negotiations are a potent opportunity to use the glow of your passion to soften the edges of those provocative financial conversations.

As a judge in divorce court, I have witnessed the devastation of people's lives—and in fact I've been married and divorced myself. I still do not have a jaundiced view about eternal love and commitment. I believe we do not have to suspend reason or romance to live a successful life with someone we love.

FINANCIAL ADVISOR TERRY SAVAGE: VIEW FROM THE BOTTOM LINE

Eventually, it's mostly about the money. Even if money is not at the heart of your differences, it is likely to be the scorecard for the dissolution of your relationship. And along the way, money often becomes the proxy for power within the relationship. Money can also be a significant force for good in your combined financial future, since two can truly live more cheaply than one—and you can save and invest the difference!

For better or for worse, two individuals are very unlikely to have the same relationship with money. And if you don't recognize those differences, and plan ahead to deal with them, money can drive a powerful wedge between the two of you, no matter how much you profess to love each other.

Your money differences may spring from long-held values or fears. Or money disagreements may arise because of financial disparity, either in income or assets. Money is a finite commodity, while your love is supposed to be infinite. Money can be tracked as it comes in and goes out, while your love is amorphous. Money lends itself to addition and subtraction, multiplication and division, while your love is supposed to remain whole and untouched.

Perhaps for all those reasons, money has the potential to become a bloody battleground in your relationship. Yet, if you are aware of the potential, you can create money strategies that are designed to bypass and avoid confrontation. You can anticipate areas of financial disagreement and structure a plan that foresees conflict and replaces it with automatic money redirection. In short, if you confront money issues in advance, you can defuse them, and even turn them to the advantage of your relationship.

> *Money has the potential to become a bloody battleground in your relationship.*

INSURANCE FOR YOUR RELATIONSHIP

Life is full of risks. That's what makes it so interesting. No matter how well you plan and how much you hope for a certain outcome, there is always the element of chance, of the unknown. Nowhere is that more true than when you decide to get married or live together. It's a big risk, in many ways.

If you took all the risk out of life, it just wouldn't be fun. But some risks are so substantial that it's prudent to insure against the possibilities—even if the risk seems remote. That's particularly true of financial risks.

Your home is one of the largest purchases you'll make in your lifetime. You invest your own money, and you borrow more. So you insure against the possibility of fire or wind damage or flood, no matter how small the chance of these occurrences. You can wish, hope, and pray that your home will stay safe, but you insure it against a costly disaster.

Similarly, if you have a car, you're likely to have auto insurance to protect not only against damage to your vehicle, but against your liability if someone else is hurt in an accident where you could be found even partly at fault. You know you're a good driver, but you want to protect against the consequences of your mistake—or someone else's error.

All that brings us to the reason you must have a prenuptial agreement before you get married or enter into a civil union, or create a cohabitation agreement if you are planning to live together. While the odds of your house burning down or your car crashing might be slim, the odds of your marriage or relationship failing are far greater. And just as with a fire or accident, all your prayers and desires to escape this risk will not change the odds.

Every day, I receive e-mails and read blog posts from people who are caught in relationships that have soured because of financial issues. A spender marries a saver—and right away, you have problems. While you can't change your partner's basic

A spender marries a saver—and right away, you have problems.

money mentality, you can set up systems and define rules that allow you to live in harmony—and financial security. But those plans are best made before unexpected circumstances, or your partner's actions, create a deal-ending conflict. You'll find the specifics later in this book.

A written agreement is insurance against a catastrophic ending to your relationship. I can tell you from personal experience that, while it sounds unromantic, it is realistic—and it can make a divorce far less painful. In my own experience, divorce was made easier by having an agreement that left no debate about finances. Now, as I live in a long-term relationship, we have chosen an arrangement that respects our individual lives and our grown children.

DEFYING THE ODDS

Don't consider the New Love Deal a bet against your relationship. In fact, if you're superstitious, you might consider it a document designed to ward off failure. It's an old saying: chance favors the well prepared. If you've both considered the downside and organized your minds—and your finances—to deal with that risk in advance, you're definitely ready to start off your relationship with optimism.

Of course, a prenuptial or cohabitation agreement is not only about finances. And it's not only for those who come into the relationship with uneven assets or income. Many prenuptial agreements provide for issues far beyond those related to money—ranging from the religious upbringing of children to spelling out where the couple will vacation or which set of parents will be included in holiday plans. While those agreed-upon preferences may not be binding in court, a divorce court judge is likely to use your agreement to help decide issues that impact your children.

Primarily, though, your agreement will revolve around financial issues, such as division of property obtained during the marriage or relationship and protection of property owned before you married or started living together. Those are the most contentious to deal with if things don't work out. And these are the "deal points" most amenable to simple decisions and plans—if the alternatives are considered *before* the participants become adversaries.

Perhaps the solution is as simple as a life insurance policy designed to fund future promises. It could be an automatic payroll deduction for separate retirement plan savings or for a joint emergency fund. Or it might be as complex as preparing an estate plan that uses trusts to provide for a new spouse, as well as children from a previous marriage. Those are some of the solutions we'll provide later in this book, along with a path to organizing your individual and combined finances to help build financial security.

But it all starts with a discussion about the unspoken fears of divorce, breakup, or death—and the fear of financial ruin. Only then will you have a forum for creating a written plan that is both acceptable and fair to each.

Defining Fairness

The word *fairness* may mean different things to each party—and eventually to a divorce court judge. Fairness is not synonymous with equality. But it is far easier to define *fair* when both parties are most concerned with the other's well-being—which is before the split takes place. And you can be sure that if the financial aspects of a relationship are not seen as fair from the start, you are building in resentments that will surface in the future.

There is no one perfect recipe for a fair financial agreement. It all depends on circumstances—and feelings. Fairness in dividing assets in a relationship that terminates without children is certainly far different than in a separation where children are involved. Fairness where a couple comes into a relationship or marriage with equal assets may be redefined if one stops working and accumulating retirement assets in order to care for children.

Don't confuse financial fairness with equality. Your written agreement is not an "equalization" of either wealth or power. Far too often, these two issues are confused, with money conferring unequal power to one party over the other. But true balance in a relationship depends on two self-confident adults who agree to mutually respect each other. Money only becomes a sign of power when respect, and self-respect, are imperiled.

How do you create that financial balance when you are two different people, have differing perspectives on money, and perhaps different priorities about spending and saving? We will take you step-by-step through the process of creating an ongoing financial plan that makes each of you comfortable and will serve as a basis for dealing with inevitable disagreements.

CREATING THE NEW LOVE DEAL: TRUST AND TALK

The creation of the Love Deal is not a sign of mistrust—either of your relationship or your belief in happy endings. It is an acknowledgment of the realities and risks. It is also a testament to the strength of your relationship and the fact that you can discuss these issues without fear of destroying your feelings for each other.

It can be a living, growing document that removes the threat of financial power as a weapon in your inevitable disagreements.

Your agreement is not merely an advance division of either money or power. Instead, properly created, it can be a living, growing document that removes the threat of financial power as a weapon in your inevitable disagreements. The agreement allows your relationship to flourish without fear of the unknown and grow without concern over downside risk.

Your legal agreement can, and should, be flexible—so it can adjust to fit future needs. Percentages of assets may be scheduled to scale up as a marriage or relationship grows in longevity or as circumstances change. Children, health issues, or business failure may complicate an agreement that does not look far enough into the future and is not flexible enough to anticipate issues that are beyond our control.

Certainly, it's difficult to define an appropriate deal that will reflect changes in income and circumstances that take place during the marriage or relationship—whether it's the accumulation of wealth or financial disaster. Our recent economic woes clearly demonstrate the importance of discussing finances and money attitudes. That's why you need guidelines and professional help to create your agreement.

Yes, your Love Deal is about financial planning. And you'll want the best advice to guide you through a process that can be clouded by emotion, just as you want the best investment advice or tax advice. But first you need to understand the basics and the potential solutions, so you can judge the advice you're given. After all, it's your relationship and your future at stake.

And a final reminder: creating your written Love Deal is not an adversarial process, nor should it be rushed. Just as you don't purchase life insurance on your deathbed or fire insurance when you smell smoke, you must organize this "relationship insurance" well in advance of your wedding day or the day you sign a lease together and move in.

Creating your Love Deal is not something to dread. It is a joint exploration of the best possible outcome. The actual process of discussing "what happens if" and "whose money will be spent on what" will lead you to a more realistic relationship and a better financial future.

I'm a firm believer that having a written agreement is indeed the best way to prevent failure of your relationship and ensure the success of your most optimistic plans and dreams. That's the Savage Truth.

Just as you don't purchase life insurance on your deathbed or fire insurance when you smell smoke, you must organize this "relationship insurance" well in advance of your wedding day or the day you sign a lease together and move in.

WE AGREE:
GEMMA, MICHELE, AND TERRY

While it is clear that we all come to this topic from very different backgrounds, our accumulated experience results in a unanimous commitment to helping you establish a firm foundation for your relationship.

We know that the best possible protection for those who are living together is shockingly similar to the best possible protection for marrying couples—a written agreement. That advice extends to same-sex couples, seniors weighing remarriage, and roommates sharing a first apartment.

In an effort to address the confusion about how to view and handle the creation of such a document, the three of us have formed an alliance dedicated to unraveling all the misconceptions about those agreements. We will give you specific information and suggested solutions to the issues that inevitably arise. We also explore the complicated perceptual issues around the idea of financial self-protection in the context of romance and marriage.

We agree that the best way to ensure a long-lasting and romantic relationship is to plan ahead. Let's get started.

Chapter 1:

HAPPILY EVER AFTER – A HOLLYWOOD FABLE

We get most of our romantic illusions—good and bad—from Hollywood. Indeed, there are lessons to be learned from those romantic experiences, especially those that take place offscreen.

There actually is a definition of "Hollywood marriage," and it is not a marriage made in heaven—or even in Hollywood. The phrase has come to mean the opposite of "happily ever after." In fact, it is now defined as "a short-lived and unhappy union."

Why should we care about these marriages and their divorce dramas? Because some of the best life lessons we can learn are from the movies and their stars. *The War of the Roses* is the quintessential bad divorce movie, and it still gets play today in divorce courts and mediation sessions. Michael Douglas and Kathleen Turner at least showed us what we don't want.

The fact that a really good divorce movie has yet to be made contributes to our national paranoia: if Hollywood cannot do it well, who can? A movie about prenuptial agreements, titled *Intolerable Cruelty*, tried to make light of seduction and cynicism, but didn't get much traction. Sex, money, and betrayal are just too serious for most of us to take lightly—even in other people's lives.

Say "Hollywood marriage" to people over fifty and they will think of Elizabeth Taylor or Marilyn Monroe and their legendary multiple marriages. But today the phrase will evoke Kim Kardashian, Katy Perry, Heidi Klum, Britney Spears, Tom Cruise, Arnold Schwarzenegger, or Charlie Sheen, to name but a few whose divorces made headlines.

Obviously, while times have changed, the Hollywood concept of a short, unhappy marriage still exists, but perhaps in hypershort space. And the most fascinating in Hollywood are those who don't marry, but manage to maintain a relationship for years. Think Brad Pitt and Angelina Jolie. Or Kurt Russell and Goldie Hawn, together for more than thirty years!

At least for Elizabeth Taylor's last divorce and Kim Kardashian's short-lived marriage, the lesson was the same: protect your assets with an agreement. Elizabeth Taylor learned that lesson the hard way after numerous marriages and divorces. Kim Kardashian allegedly learned it only by reluctantly deferring to her advisors. In both cases, it's conservatively estimated that tens of millions of dollars were preserved for the star/personality with the help of a written Love Deal in the form of a prenuptial agreement.

Its said that the lessons that cost the most teach the most. An expensive divorce or split-up is one lesson you don't want to learn the hard way.

It's said that the lessons that cost the most teach the most. An expensive divorce or split-up is one lesson you don't want to learn the hard way.

LA Stories

If you believe what you read in the tabloids, stars appear to have a high level of ambivalence about the Love Deal. Even when they admit to prenuptials, they are uniquely creative in their terms.

Reportedly, Catherine Zeta-Jones and Michael Douglas have an agreement that compensates her almost $3 million a year for every year they stay together, and she gets a substantial bonus if he cheats. She is a beautiful, successful woman who married a much older successful man. To have and nurture children and to support his career, she necessarily slowed down her own—so it appears she decided to save through the mechanism of a pre-nuptial, while she spent some of her youth and career potential on Michael Douglas. Ironically, she later starred in *Intolerable Cruelty*, where the woman she played seemed to be into prenuptial agreement avoidance—and was far less grounded than Ms. Zeta-Jones is in real life.

Allegedly, Katie Holmes took a page from the Zeta-Jones playbook and crafted a similar deal for herself. That prenuptial agreement could have been one reason Katie's public exit from her involvement with Tom Cruise ended so swiftly and without a court battle. It probably also did not hurt that Katie's father is an attorney, who could advise her on any deal.

Both deals had a reported sunset clause—they would expire after ten years, and then the law of their jurisdiction would take over. Since both women live in California, which is a community property state, that clause could have meant even more equity for each woman after the "sunset." However, Katie Holmes exited after only five years, taking the benefit of her bargain and her daughter with her.

The split between Gwyneth Paltrow and her rocker husband, Chris Martin, is but the latest to play out in the headlines before it moves to the courthouse. Perhaps time will reveal whether a prenuptial agreement will preserve their respective fortunes — and facilitate their public pledge to coparent their two children in an amiable manner. On her website, GOOP, Paltrow spoke of a new concept she called "conscious uncoupling." We wish them the best, and we hope that their plans to remain close friends and good parents are not disrupted by disputes that could have been resolved in advance.

Kudos to those successful people when they insist on prenuptial protection as a part of their Love Deal. But do they have more to lose than you do? Just because they are wealthy and their lives play out in public does not mean that the issues surrounding divorce or separation are any less painful. They just have the benefit of smart advisors, if they pay attention. And in the end, that advice can mitigate a portion of the pain.

There's no reason you shouldn't benefit from the same kind of planning. Realistically, most ordinary men or women will have the same potential problems—just on a smaller, less expensive stage!

There is nothing wrong in evaluating the contribution and costs of each partner. Is it crass or just practical to recognize the give-and-take in every relationship? In the California entertainment business, there is no clearer lesson than the short-term shelf life of youth and beauty. Young, beautiful women who drop out of a starring career, or even drop back, would be foolish indeed not to assess the financial losses involved—as well as the upside.

MONEY TALKS

In Hollywood lore, the have-not in the relationship was called a gold digger. But in truth, the person with greater financial assets clearly valued something about the other. That's part of the attraction. And that early stage of attraction is when the relationship is most balanced. Perhaps now that the wealthier person in a relationship is just as likely to be a woman as a man, recognition of what each person brings to the relationship, including energy and health, will be more appropriately acknowledged.

And sometimes the financial relationships reverse in mid-marriage. Just consider the marriage of Demi Moore and Ashton Kutcher. At the time of their marriage in September 2005, Moore was at the height of her Hollywood career. They separated in 2011, and Kutcher went on to star in a popular TV sitcom—and to become a very successful tech investor. The divorce dragged on publicly and was settled just days before the stock of Twitter went public in late 2013, at a very high valuation.

It is rumored that not only did Kutcher become an early and popularly followed celebrity on Twitter, but he had invested in the company through an earlier private equity deal. If his holdings were valued after the stock soared in its public debut, Kutcher would have owed a great deal more to Demi, possibly fueling his last-minute settlement.

Another New Love Deal lesson might be that while we all choose to ignore red flags and love whomever we want, the help of a written agreement can soften the economic blow if a red flag blows up in our face. It seems obvious that Sandra Bullock would vouch for that principle. Nicole Kidman's prenuptial agreement (until death or divorce shall part her from music star Keith Urban) allegedly penalizes certain behaviors.

While Hollywood entertains us on-screen, it also gives us life lessons in relationship breakups. One more lesson: even short-term marriages can result in costly breakups, absent a prenup.

Not only the *Titanic*, but its movie director, ended up in dangerous waters. A backstory of the making of that movie involved the allegation that James Cameron, who directed it, fell hard for one of its young stars. Sadly for everyone at the time, he was newly married to Linda Hamilton, the actress of *Terminator* fame. The tabloids reported that Hamilton walked away with half his profits—reportedly $50 million—from the blockbuster *Titanic* after only a two-year marriage.

If true, it would indicate they did not have any binding financial agreement for their unplanned marital disaster. Cameron is creative and resourceful, and his *Avatar* has exceeded his *Titanic* success. But one never knows when one has made one's last great fortune. So the New Love Deal lesson here is that you have to be willing to live with the consequences of your own actions —or inactions. That can be expensive.

You have to be willing to live with the consequences of your own actions —or inactions.

Another famous director, Steven Spielberg, had a $100 million divorce after a relatively short marriage. When he married actress Amy Irving, they did sign an agreement, but four years later, when they were divorcing, she challenged its legalities. The agreement was apparently scribbled on a napkin, which, in and of itself, might not

If you want an agreement to be enforceable, do it right.

have invalidated it. However, at the time of the alleged scribbling, Ms. Irving had no attorney and thus the "agreement" failed. Easy Love Deal lesson: if you want an agreement to be enforceable, do it right.

CINDERELLA STORIES

Long ago and far away, a movie star named Grace Kelly married a prince named Rainier. The "fairy tale" lasted for many years until her untimely accidental death. It is said that her prenuptial agreement would have required her to surrender custody of any children if the marriage failed.

Other actual princess experiences include those of Princess Di, with whose story we are all too familiar and whose divorce settlement before her sad demise seemed to be "underwhelming" at a reported £20 million.

Love Deal lessons learned: even princesses—or some princes—do not live happily ever after.

Clearly, love is not enough! We all secretly want to believe that "All You Need Is Love" à la the Beatles' song. Could there be a more spectacular example of the fact that love is not enough than Sir Paul McCartney's marriage to Heather Mills? There was more than enough money to go around. They were the international paparazzi's dream couple. He wrote a song called "Heather," naming her the "queen of his heart." Famously then and infamously later, they did not have a prenuptial agreement.

After four years of "wedded bliss," a few years of sour notes, two years of divorce wars, and one child, Heather was awarded $48.6 million. Without a prenuptial, she attained a court-ordered divorce payout. It is tempting to speculate as to what would have happened had they reached an agreement before they were married. Sir Paul's fortune, in boxcar numbers, is estimated to be between $800 million and $1.6 billion. What Lady Heather did get, she might have gotten under any circumstances, since it was such a small percentage of his ever-increasing wealth.

What she and Sir Paul both lost, however, may have been priceless. Their respective reputations were attacked by the press, and their daughter will grow up with that legacy. Prior to their marriage, he might have agreed to provide his wife with several million for every year of marriage and perhaps a baby bonus. It seems likely, because that is not an unusual approach to "star-nups." What is certain is that the child born to Paul and Heather would have had a less public childhood if her parents had divorced less hostilely. Their privacy and dignity would not have been tabloid talk, fueled by the media circus surrounding their financial warfare.

Now, McCartney has married again. Dare we wish him happiness and, in the same sentence, hope he has a prenup this time?

One of our own "almost royals," Jacqueline Kennedy Onassis, also had a less-than-fairy-tale ending. After the assassination of her (and America's) young prince, John F. Kennedy, and after suffering the murder of her brother-in-law Robert, Jackie Kennedy took her children and fled the unsafe aura of what had formerly been her Camelot. She married a Greek shipping tycoon named Aristotle Onassis, who ensconced them on a private island and in a golden life.

This alleged prince tuned out to be a frog, and their life together was mostly a Greek tragedy. Shortly before his death, rumors were that they were divorcing. Because she was a non-Greek spouse, her leverage was limited, and her settlement with his estate primarily inherited by his daughter, Christina Onassis, was reported to be $26 million. She endured and continued as an American icon; she was reborn as a stellar editor and remained so until the next sad chapters of her life. Only she could have judged whether she made a rewarding Love Deal.

LOVE LESSONS ON AND OFF THE COURT

From the sports world comes an unexpectedly expensive ending. Allegedly, Michael Jordan and his wife had a prenuptial financial agreement that divided everything acquired during their marriage fifty-fifty. Since they reside in a state that provides for equitable distribution, and the presumptive starting point for equitable distribution is fifty-fifty anyway, one wonders why Michael Jordan was not playing more "defense" in his prenuptial agreement.

With this particular Love Deal and his phenomenal success, his divorce was reportedly one of the most expensive at $168 million to his former wife, Juanita. It was, however, discreet and paparazzi-free, so from that perspective, the prenuptial agreement could be considered a success. When Jordan married his second wife, Yvette

Prieto, in 2013, after four years of living together, it would not be surprising if they executed a more protective prenup than he gave his first wife.

Another basketball player wasn't so "lucky." Kobe Bryant's exploits were well publicized. But lacking a prenup, his wife, Vanessa, stuck it out for ten years and two months—just past the statutory limit for California marriages to qualify for a fifty-fifty community property split. Kobe had all the moves on the basketball court, but without a prenup, he had no play in divorce court. Vanessa's child support alone is reported to be $40 million!

Another sports figure in the marital financial news was Alex Rodriguez, the highly paid baseball player, who had signed a ten-year, $275 million contract—and allegedly promptly started an affair with Madonna. Within five days of that reported tryst, his wife of five years sued him for emotional abandonment, an extramarital affair, and other wrongs—demanding a share of the big money in his new contract. While financial details have not been revealed, A-Rod has said his fortune was spared because of their prenuptial agreement.

Speaking of behavioral issues, Tiger Woods also had a prenuptial agreement, but reportedly overpaid to have at least a semidiscreet ending. Reportedly, ex-wife Elin Nordegren walked away with $100 million. While the prenuptial agreement was not the end of the story, it did help to contain what could have been nuclear fallout.

LOVE LESSONS FROM BIG BUSINESSMEN AND BIG DIVORCES

Presumably, some wealthy businessmen had no written Love Deals because they married before attaining such great fortunes that a prenup was an obvious necessity. That must be the Rupert Murdoch story. He and his second wife, Anna Torv, married in 1967 and divorced in 1999, when Murdoch became involved with the much younger Wendi Deng, a Chinese business executive at one of his companies. Divorcing Anna was estimated to cost Murdoch $1.7 billion Aussie dollars, suggesting the Australian media giant made no cautionary prenuptial agreement—or that he was very anxious to marry Deng, which he did less than a month later.

Did Murdoch learn a lesson from that expensive divorce? Did Deng take note of what happened to her predecessor? One hopes so, because in June 2013, the eighty-two-year-old Murdoch filed for divorce from Deng, after thirteen years of marriage and two daughters. Media reports have speculated on what would become of Murdoch's reputed $11.2 billion fortune, and with good reason. Two months after the split was announced, Deng hired a new and famously aggressive divorce attorney. It's unknown whether the couple had a prenup, but if the litigation heats up, we hope their Love Deal was signed in indelible ink and followed all proper procedures.

A successful businessman who also seems to have been less than savvy in love is Jack Welch. Granted, he was smart enough to have a prenuptial agreement in his second marriage, but he also allowed it to fully expire after ten years. He might have been wiser to negotiate a lengthier deal with a less costly "sunset." After thirteen years of marriage to his second wife, Jack admittedly fell in love with a divorced editor of the *Harvard Business Review* named Suzy. She was interviewing him on his many successes, and according to both of them, "sparks flew" from the very beginning.

It wasn't just the money, which a longer and more structured prenuptial agreement might have preserved. What really suffered in the messy divorce were his reputation and his perquisites from General Electric, which his second wife brought to light in the litigation. The ensuing scandal was public and predatory, and painted him as greedy at best. It also put his new wife's ethics and journalistic integrity up for intense scrutiny.

With a different or only partial expiration date on his prenuptial agreement, Jack Welch would have been able to "fall in love" without so much public second-guessing about his and her private and professional decisions, and presumably with a better managed and more manageable settlement.

POLITICS AND PRENUPTIALS

How liberated we are as a voting electorate is evidenced by our presidential candidates and their finances. John Kerry was and is married to the heiress to the H. J. Heinz fortune. He has candidly disclosed that he signed a prenuptial agreement protecting her inheritance. But when he ran for president, in addition to other campaign slurs he endured, there were articles and slogans written stating that "if his own wife would not trust him, neither should the country."

Fast-forward to 2008, and we find that this time, it was the Republican candidate, John McCain, who executed a prenuptial agreement when he married his wife, Cindy, almost thirty years ago. That is probably why McCain really could not answer the question as to how many houses they have. He would have had to check with his lawyer first! Nevertheless, the presence of private financial agreements for men at the top of two tickets has to be evidence of the public acceptance of this rising phenomenon.

Clearly, this New Love Deal takeaway is that more and more couples are engaging in the private ordering of their finances. It is apparently becoming politically correct.

YOUR LOVE DEAL

The stories in this chapter are the ones that make headlines because of the big names and the big money involved. But are their hearts any larger than yours? Were their dreams any less meaningful when they entered into marriage or started living together? Was it easier to decide child custody or who would get the dog? Were their emotions any less seared because of the amount of money involved?

Split-ups hurt. And who can measure another's pain? Many splitting couples report that they are so ambushed by either the divorce itself or the legal process that they never have time to do anything except to react emotionally—and sometimes disastrously.

What the stars and certain captains of industry illustrate is that negotiating ahead of time and "just in case" is a much safer proposal. So read on to learn about the ways to protect your relationship from the financial and emotional devastation of the stories illustrated here.

LESSONS LEARNED

So, now that you've salivated over these details of marriage, divorce, and separation of the rich and famous, what Love Deal lessons can you learn from such royal and rarefied air? For indeed, though you and your partner only dream of accumulating a tidbit of this bounty, the same rules and issues apply. Most revolve around finances, and the issues of obligation and loyalty when love no longer rules, but legal documents determine outcomes.

A few lessons on Love Deals do come to mind from these very public examples:

1. No matter how rich or powerful the couple is, ending a relationship is painful. But it is far less so if you have a prenup.

2. If you marry someone with overreaching fame or power and money, it is smart to know what the financial end might look like while you are still at the beginning—and at your most beguiling. And if you don't think you have the power within your relationship to request a written agreement, you will really know what "powerless" means as you move ahead without a Love Deal.

3. If you have been or plan to be in the public eye for any reason, a written agreement can protect your privacy—both financial and emotional—and your children's privacy, too. Up to a point, of course. Paparazzi still follow Katie Homes and her daughter, Suri. And one day, Suri will have to consider her own Love Deal. But that's a long time off; meanwhile, her smart, deal-oriented parents came to a quick and private settlement.

4. If you do a financial agreement with a termination or "sunset" date, should there be some written expectation of "good behavior" after? In other words, if the financial limits expire after ten years, shouldn't there be a requirement of discretion for even additional financial reward? Why make terminating the deal a goal instead of a pathway to the future?

Chapter 2:

LET'S MAKE A PRENUP DEAL

In this chapter, we'll give you some background on the evolution of the prenup agreement and its position in our society, as well as the legal requirements of a valid agreement—and an idea of some of the key ingredients in the prenup you might want to create. Many of the same concepts apply to cohabitation agreements and same-sex couple arrangements, as you'll see in chapter 4.

IN THE BEGINNING

In the beginning, there was Adam and Eve. A woman's biblical role was to marry and bear and nurture children; a man's role was to care for his wife (or wives) and all their children. Somewhere along the historical way, man's primary role became to control the family assets. Ever after the Garden of Eden, marriage and money have been linked.

For a long span of history, marriages were usually arranged by parents for practical reasons—substituting parental judgment for human emotion. But even biblical history is filled with the hope and poetry of love. The Song of Songs 8:6–7 declares: "For love is as strong as death, its jealousy unyielding as the grave, it burns like blazing fire, like a mighty flame, many waters cannot quench love; rivers cannot wash it away. If one were to give all the wealth of his house for love, it would be utterly scorned." True love was universally recognized as priceless.

LOVE AND MARRIAGE

Marriage evolved through the centuries to the mid-1900s model of monogamous marriage with choices made by the couples themselves based solely on love. The quintessential American nuclear family became the be-all and end-all and every couple's expectation. Divorce was socially unacceptable, and for the most part, your spousal choices were irrevocable.

Fast-forward just fifty years—divorce went from being unacceptable to expectable. And here we are! Approximately 50 percent of marriages will end in divorce unless couples do something to change their own probabilities.

PRENUPTIAL AGREEMENTS THROUGH TIME

The history of prenuptial agreements has not been pretty. As mentioned in the introduction, traditionally they have been for the very rich and designed to keep them very rich. It was the Golden Rule in its most impure form: whoever had the gold ruled. The contracts were signed by the less affluent person, who fervently hoped that

The history of prenuptial agreements has not been pretty.

16

love would prevail over law. These "deals" were signed before there were children, financial reverses, or health issues. Since one party had no bargaining power and no one had a crystal ball, they were rarely, if ever, "fair."

Luckily for some, up until the early 1980s, the court system recognized the uneven playing field. Where there was a prenuptial agreement in a divorce, the judge would/could take a second look and see how life really turned out. It was comforting to know that if you felt forced to make a bad deal, the court might help rescue you later. The problem was that often the court did not take that second look or you could not afford the litigation it required. Signing away some of or all your rights was and always will be a risky business.

Uniform Premarital Agreement Act

To the largest extent possible, even that potential "rescue" is no longer available in more modern times. Pursuant to the Uniform Premarital Agreement Act, created in 1983, gradually adopted in twenty-six states and DC, and followed to a degree in many states even if not formally adopted, the emphasis is now on *procedural fairness* and not the substantive fairness of the deal.

If proper procedures were available, such as separate counsel and full disclosure of assets and income, whether you did or did not take advantage of these procedures, the deal you make is the deal you take!

Even before the widespread enactment of that act, the law was harsher than most people realized. One woman in Illinois, who was worth about $5,000, married a man worth about $6 million. He made a full and complete disclosure of his income and assets.

They had been together for eleven years, married for most of them. In court, the wife testified that her husband told her the agreement was "just a formality."

Against her lawyer's advice, she signed the agreement literally the day before the wedding. It provided her with half of anything that was put in joint names, and $1,400 a month in support for six years. As a result, after almost a decade of marriage to a multimillionaire, she received a total of $201,000 and six years of taxable maintenance worth about another $90,000.

Even though their agreement also had a provision that her maintenance could be modified upward if untoward catastrophic circumstances occurred—which would subject her to abject poverty or make her a public charge—the court said she had "enough." She received in total less than 5 percent of the assets after nearly ten years of marriage. There was no "rescue" for her. She spent ten years of her life in and grew accustomed to a lifestyle she could never again provide for herself. But the court said she had to stick to her original deal.

In another landmark case in Georgia, a court held that the wife's premarital pregnancy was not "duress." Even the husband's failure to disclose over $500,000 in annual income was not sufficient to undo the premarital agreement. In that same case, the wife had only a high school education, while the husband had a college education, a successful business, and was worth $8.5 million.

During the trial, the wife testified that the husband had assured her that the agreement was "just a formality" and that he would always take care of her. The couple signed a prenup nine days before the wedding. She saw an attorney who did not have time to review the document. She negotiated some life insurance and slightly better alimony for herself than her husband proposed, and signed the deal. After eighteen years of marriage and four children, the husband was worth $22.7 million—and the wife was held to her prenuptial deal of $2,900 a month for four years. Her husband kept all the assets.

The moral of this story is that neither a man nor a woman can rely on the "just a formality, dear" reassurance.

UNDERSTANDING THE PRENUP GUIDELINES

Before a couple can make any kind of deal, they not only have to open their hearts and minds but also understand the legal rules of engagement. Here's what you need to know before you start:

- The law can and does vary from jurisdiction to jurisdiction. Even if the wording of the statutes appears the same, some states might interpret it differently than others. Some judges in the same state might apply the same law differently. That's why you need local counsel if you want to make a binding agreement.

- In many, if not most, states, if a prenup was written according to state law, the "fairness" of the results will not be second-guessed by the courts. It does not matter whose business went up or down, whose health improved or declined, or how many children you have. That is why you have to define fairness for yourselves.

- Each of you must make a full disclosure of your assets, income, and debts.

- Each of you should have your own attorney.

- You need time, trust, and techniques to negotiate a fair agreement.

- If you have doubts about the agreement or its terms, decline to sign. It doesn't matter if the wedding is the next day, or you are pregnant, or you are madly in love. If you still have doubts, *don't sign*—even if your beloved says it's "just a formality; I will always take care of you," and even if you have five hundred people coming tomorrow for a star-studded ceremony to be followed by a formal dinner and fireworks.

As we are envisioning the New Love Deal, these written agreements will be the very foundation of your future together. *You do not want to build on shaky ground.*

OF LOVE AND LAW

At first blush, "laying down the future law" of a relationship seems to create infinite possibilities—she or he will never be allowed to gain weight; she or he will always change any diaper; in-laws will never/always be welcome; there will never/always be pets in the house; it will be an SOD (sex-on-demand) household; and the relationship will always be picture-perfect and fidelity maintained or else fines and bonuses will be paid by the offender.

Believe it or not, for certain celebrities, at least some of these clauses have been included in their prenuptial contract. But for the rest of us, the financial bottom line will be the baseline for our agreements. That is a good thing because, while the "cosmetic and control clauses" are worth discussing between the two of you just so you know what matters to each of you, their legal enforceability is unlikely. However, we would be willing to wager the penalty for "playing around" has been quietly paid by some of the rich and famous to avoid embarrassment.

READY, SET, GO CREATE YOUR DEAL

So, here's what you know. It's smart to create a legally enforceable prenuptial agreement now, before you get married. You know you each need a competent attorney to represent you, and you know you must make full disclosure of all your assets.

But you don't want to simply hand over the process to the attorneys. They know the law, but they don't know your hopes and desires, and they don't know the dynamics of your relationship. They know the issues that will matter in the long run, but without your guidance, they're likely to insert provisions that don't matter to you—and might create unnecessary hostility.

It's up to you to give the attorneys some guidance about what you want in the agreement. That's why we created the list below, for the two of you to discuss before you meet with them. In later chapters we expand and explain some of these financial and legal concepts, so you can have an understanding of what's involved and how it will protect each of you.

One of the first issues to consider is the *trigger* for your agreement to spring into action—a point in time when the provisions begin to apply. It could be when one party moves out of the shared residence, or when one files for divorce. Or the trigger could simply be a written letter stating that one of you believes the relationship has ended, and that it's time to begin implementing your agreement.

That's a sobering thought. When entering into an important relationship, none of us wants to consider what the end will look like. But once again, we want to prepare you—just in case. If the end does come, the goal is to make that transition as painless as possible, avoiding bitterness that destroys the memories of happier times.

To get you started on the prenup process, we've created a list of things that your prenup could address. If your relationship needs additional categories, feel free to add them. If each of you takes these topics and prioritizes your list, then shares it with your beloved, the framework of your agreement will start to take shape!

Top Prenuptial Issues

✓ Asset division upon divorce or death

✓ Maintenance (alimony) if the relationship does not work out—how much and how long?

✓ Financial support during proceedings in case of divorce

✓ Ongoing money management plan during the relationship

✓ Debt—whose is it, and how to manage it

✓ Financial responsibilities from prior marriages, including child support, alimony

✓ Keeping current assets (including inheritances) separate from marital property

✓ Gifts you give to each other

✓ Income tax payments and apportionment, joint tax returns

✓ Retirement savings—accumulation, distribution

✓ Life insurance

✓ Creation of new estate plan, reflecting your prenup agreement provisions

✓ Ownership of business interests either or both of you may have

A second tier of concerns is the child-related constellation. This set of issues is "second" not because they matter less, but because they are less likely to be enforceable.

No matter what the two of you decide regarding child-related issues, the courts are the ultimate "guardian" of your child or children and can override your premarital discretion/direction, particularly if either of you challenges them later. Be that as it may, the child-related discussions are important and instructive for the sake of your future as a couple.

✓ Do you both anticipate having children?

✓ Do you envision at least one stay-at-home parent?

✓ How will you handle religious upbringing, if at all?

✓ If the marriage should not work out, should custody be only to one of you or joint to both of you, and if joint, what is the schedule for parenting that you will decide to divide?

✓ What are your college funding plans?

✓ What arrangements have you made for support of the child on dissolution or death?

✓ Is there a bonus payment for having children?

Yes, as you'll see later, there are some other social provisions you could insert in your agreement. But if they are too frivolous, such language could lead a judge to reject those provisions. Stick to the basics listed above as you approach your deal.

Getting to and through these value-oriented discussions with humor, grace, and honesty is not easy, and we fully acknowledge the challenge. But reviewing the issues on the list can open up hearts, minds, and a productive dialogue. It's time to get started!

Chapter 3:

MOVING IN—
THE COHABITATION DEAL

Cohabitation is on the rise for many reasons—the greatest of these is divorce. Scratch the psychological surface of committed cohabiters, and you will often find a bad divorce—their parents', their own, their best friend's, or just what they see in the media. Cohabiters have seen the pain, the complications, and the government involvement in maintaining and/or ending a personal relationship, and find them all to be distasteful and avoidable. "Just live together" is the seemingly simple solution.

Cohabitation is on the rise for many reasons—the greatest of these is divorce

We sometimes choose cohabitation simply to delay the legal entanglements of marriage and to avoid the complications of a breakup. Living together carries with it the illusion of traveling light and packing up your electric toothbrush and your flat screen if the relationship does not work out. It also appears to be more romantic because the only thing holding the two of you together is love unchained by legal commitment. The problem is that cohabitation is anything but simple, and, in some states, it can be positively dangerous to your wealth.

No one had heard the word *palimony* until it was coined in the split-up of Hollywood actor Lee Marvin and his longtime live-in lover, Michelle Triola. They lived together for six years but never married, and the relationship ended in 1970. She agreed to accept payment of $833 per month while she tried to restart her career. But when the checks stopped coming, she sued. Famous Hollywood divorce attorney Marvin Mitchelson came up with the idea to sue for half of everything Lee Marvin had earned during their years together. She would have won $1.8 million—a huge sum at the time.

The case went all the way to the state supreme court, which granted an unmarried cohabitant the right to sue. She was ultimately awarded a small amount, and the award was subsequently overturned. But the right to alimony for an unmarried partner was established. And Marvin coined the word palimony, which has struck financial fear into the hearts of cohabiting partners ever since.

FIRST COMES LOVE, THEN COMES COHABITATION

There are practical reasons for living together while you plan the wedding, combine your assets, and ease into a blended life. But if you live together for too long, research shows that you may jeopardize your finances and even, ultimately, your marriage when and if you do choose to marry. How ironic. We all know at least one couple who were together for several happy years, married at leisure, and divorced in haste.

There are many different reasons people choose living together over marriage. It doesn't have to be psychologically complicated. It just might seem "easier" than getting married. Or one partner may not be able for financial, religious, or medical reasons to secure a divorce. Perhaps they have a fear of commitment, or perhaps they want to avoid the psychological and legal discomfort that comes with tying the knot. But even if a couple chooses to "just" live together, there are legal and financial issues lurking around the relationship.

New Love Deal: Living Together Is Anything but Simple

The apparently simple societal solution of cohabitation is the proverbial can of worms stored in a Pandora's box. Living together can be a hot legal mess. The simple fact is that same-sex partners, who for the most part can only live together, are fighting for the right to marry for many reasons—but a significant one is the legal protection and predictability a marriage can offer. They have had to struggle through the pain and the complications that result from "just living together."

Living together can be a hot legal mess.

Common-Law Marriage

An old-fashioned term and little understood concept is "common-law marriage." We all have some vague notion that if you live together long enough, you may end up with a common-law marriage, with all the rights and remedies of a regular marriage. The term was first used in the nineteenth century, when it was believed that marriage was a common right of society, and not something that originated with a law of government. While it was recognized that governments have a right to regulate certain aspects of marriage (how old a person must be before marriage, marriage to cousins, and even same-sex marriage), the actual "right" to be married did not emanate from government.

Currently, fifteen states, plus the District of Columbia, have some form of recognition of common-law marriage. But, the catch is that each state defines common-law marriage somewhat differently, so you need an attorney in your state to give you the specifics. Basically, all require some aspect of the following:

- Be a resident of the state that allows common-law marriage.

- Live together for a specific period of time.

- Hold themselves publicly to being a married couple; for example, using the same last name.

The lack of specificity around common-law marriage has led to many misconceptions about the rights and duties of people who live together, in what is usually incorrectly perceived to be a common-law marriage.

Misconception #1:

If you live together for whatever is "long enough," you will have a common-law marriage with all legal protections, even if you never actually went through a ceremony.

Fact:

Very few states (and DC) even recognize such marriages formed within their jurisdiction: Alabama, Colorado, Iowa, Kansas, Montana, Oklahoma, Rhode Island, South Carolina, Texas, and Utah (to a certain extent). Five other states will recognize such a marriage only if it began before varying dates or for certain purposes: Georgia (before 1997), Idaho (before 1996), New Hampshire (only for inheritance purposes), Ohio (before 1991), and Pennsylvania (before 2005).

Once you have established such a relationship but move from one of these locations, other states will recognize the relationship under the full faith and credit clause of the US Constitution—so long as you really met all the requirements of the original state of residence.

The moral of this part of the legal living-together morass is: choose your residential state carefully if you want to eventually have the rights of a legal marriage, and avoid the above-named locations if your goal is to stay as far away from marriage as possible.

Some well-known athletes have been caught unaware of the legal dangers of long-term relationships carried on in common-law states. Many a former girlfriend or boyfriend of football or baseball stars has advanced the theory of his or her legal and financial status as a common-law spouse, whether or not he or she prevailed.

Misconception #2:

If you live together for X number of years, you automatically have a common-law marriage.

Fact:

It is not actually the set number of years that defines a common-law marriage. Instead, the basic definition is: "a positive mutual agreement, permanent and exclusive of all others, to enter into a marriage relationship, cohabitation necessary to warrant a fulfillment of necessary relationship of man and wife and an assumption of marital duties and obligations." But that definition is just the beginning of the complicated proofs you are required to present to confirm a common-law marriage. By the way, a common-law marriage is not legally available to same-sex couples in any state.

Something Old, Something New

In a different and more flamboyant era, common-law marriages were more—dare we say—"common." The famous Florenz Ziegfeld Jr., who clearly had an eye for beautiful women, allegedly had a passionate and scandalous common-law marriage to one of his protégées, Anna Held. Stan Laurel was sued by one of his (many, many) women friends on the theory that they had a common-law marriage. Even Rembrandt was said to have loved and painted a common-law wife.

Do Oprah Winfrey and Stedman Graham, who have lived together in a relationship for a quarter of a century, have a common-law marriage? They have homes in California and Illinois, states that do not recognize common-law marriage. We're guessing they do have some form of legal agreement, which limits his access to her assets, just in case!

The New Love Deal:
Consider a Cohabitation Agreement

It is harder to label the new relationship choices people are making nowadays. Marriages are kept secret, breakups are breathlessly reported by Internet sites, and Los Angeles realtors are kept busy selling houses purchased by stars who lived together for only a short time. It is said in their happy days, the beautiful actress Charlize Theron declared herself "married" to Irish actor Stuart Townsend, while allegedly simultaneously claiming there was no marriage ceremony. They could have been secretly married, or they could have been seriously committed cohabiters.

In any event, the same lifestyle choices are now available to all of us. But the myriad relationship options make these arrangements more complicated, and often create unexpected legal consequences. One answer to help ensure one's rights without a marriage license is to enter into a *conuptial* or *cohabitation* agreement.

Palimony and Promises versus Written Agreement

In the previously mentioned Marvin/Triola palimony case, Michelle Triola said she had relied on his verbal promises to care for her for the rest of her life and sought half the property acquired while they were together. But they didn't have a written contract. And oral deals are the hardest to prove, because they turn into "he said/she said."

Triola sued for nearly $2 million for "services" as his "wife" and for loss of her own career. Perhaps out of sympathy, the California court awarded a relatively small amount. But even that award was subsequently overturned on appeal because she had failed to prove the existence of any contract whatsoever.

The Marvin case recognized property rights for unmarried couples, but confused the legal landscape as to when you could and could not qualify for these rights. The reason the case and other legal opinions on the topic seem so confusing is that they reflect our deep philosophical national confusion as to what is right and wrong about granting legal rights to people who choose to live together "without benefit of marriage." The struggle is ongoing and not likely to resolve itself soon. It is fought out in civil courts (not divorce court) under the rules of contracts.

In Marvin's case, the court found that while a couple could live together, presumably have a sexual relationship, and maintain the right to have oral or written agreements between them, those agreements can be invalidated "(only) if sexual acts form an inseparable part of the consideration for the agreement." The court basically said you cannot contract with each other *for* sex, but you can contract with each other and have sex. In the end, no contract was found to exist—oral, written, or implied—and Marvin's companion lost on every theory.

When and if you are seeking palimony, an important question is where in the United States you reside. If you live in Illinois or Louisiana, public policy will not favor oral agreements or even written agreements that seem to involve a "meretricious relationship" with sexual requirements. California and other states, including New Jersey, are much more open to the concepts of the rights of the unmarried, whether or not their agreements are in writing.

Another famous California palimony case involved Martina Navratilova (the nine-time Wimbledon singles champion). A former girlfriend sued for half of Navratilova's earnings—allegedly over $1 million. She allegedly made no secret of the fact that there was dirty laundry she was prepared to air, should the case not be resolved to her satisfaction. A written conup or cohab agreement would have been the better way to end the match for both parties, and in fact for all parties who are living together. The dollar amounts and terms could have been privately agreed upon and confidentially paid.

Stay away from agreements (whether oral or written) that seem to bestow rights upon you or your partner in exchange for a marital relationship (i.e., sex) as an essential part of the "deal." And, as always, check with a local lawyer to understand your legal status and create the appropriate documentation.

What's a Cohabiting Couple to Do?

First of all, define your relationship. If you are a couple who moved in together because one or the other's lease ran out in May and the wedding isn't until September, it is probably a prenup on which you need to spend your time and attention, and not a cohabitation agreement.

If, however, you are a couple in it for the long term, then the best option for you is a carefully drawn written contract. Without something in writing, you are left to rely on what you each *thought* were the agreements you made. If and when you break up, it is unlikely you will

Without something in writing, you are left to rely on what you each thought were the agreements you made.

agree; each party will see the facts and circumstances in a way that most favors his or her own position. It is just human nature.

The financial misunderstandings are predictable if the relationship starts to slip away. Were the trips charged to one of our credit cards really intended to be paid fifty-fifty, or were they a gift from the one whose credit card bears it? What about that mortgage? Did we each really pay half, or did we just do a balancing act with expenditures that leaves one of us with a less clear paper trail as to our contributions to the relationship? Is the house titled in joint name—and who made the down payment? It's all in the legal and financial details, which must be spelled out in advance.

UNCOUPLING

The courts have methods of uncoupling these breakups, and there can be some legal hope for you even without a written agreement—but your life would be so much easier with a contract. Courts can and do use various methods to help unmarried couples solve their financial differences, depending on the facts and circumstances. If there has been a business undertaking by the two of you, or if one or the other of you has been "unjustly enriched" by the relationship, the courts may award a portion of disputed assets to reach fundamental fairness. But don't count on it!

You will be seeking legal protection, not in the divorce courts, but rather in a court of equity or law, on the theory that the two of you had a contract—whether that contract is oral, written, or implied. If the contract is written, you are safer and your relief more achievable. If the contract is oral or implied, the one seeking relief faces an uphill battle. And if you have a child together, you will also find yourself in paternity court, where the child's welfare is paramount.

Litigation is an expensive route to fairness, and one that holds no guarantees and many pitfalls. Remember, too, that in some states, the courts will do much more to protect your legal rights as a cohabitant than in others, so check with a local attorney as to the realities in your jurisdiction and be guided by that advice.

MAKING HER DAY

Clint Eastwood and Sondra Locke were a famous unmarried couple who accessed the court system more than once when unraveling their relationship. Luckily, for her at least, they lived in California where the court was sympathetic, if not totally "fair."

They met in 1975 while involved in a film called *The Outlaw Josey Wales*. As the story goes, their relationship began shortly thereafter and lasted until 1989. When they broke up, she filed a palimony suit claiming her rights in joint assets the couple accumulated during their time together.

She agreed to drop the suit when Clint Eastwood facilitated a "director's contract" for her at Warner Bros., said to be worth $1.5 million. But when Warner Bros. rejected thirty different proposals she made for films—making the alleged "deal" virtually worthless—she sued again.

In round two of their litigation, Locke sued Eastwood for career sabotage, claiming she had been offered a phantom contract by him through the Warner deal to induce her to drop her substantial palimony rights. During the trial, it became evident that—unknown to Locke—Eastwood had paid $1 million to Warner Bros. to facilitate the deal for her. Locke testified that she would never have accepted either deal had she understood Eastwood's involvement. The jury did not believe Eastwood when he said he only paid Warner Bros. to "facilitate her career." Locke might have been awarded a large sum in damages, ranging as high as $100 million, but she and Eastwood settled this phase of their dispute during the trial for an undisclosed sum.

While the end of the case clearly helped Sondra Locke "make her day," it took two lawsuits over a seven-year period for a settlement to be reached, and that was in California, which is a relatively friendly forum for live-in lovers. With a written agreement, their ending could have been more about "the good" and less about "the bad," and certainly not so ugly.

SETTING UP A COHABITATION DEAL

For any kind of cohabitation agreement, the issues are both the same and different than for married couples. As a first step, a definition of what constitutes separate property is needed.

That definition is very personal and very defining to the nature of the relationship. Everything can be defined to be separate, but then you are basically "roommates with benefits." You can decide that some things are separate, and others are or will become joint property as you move forward. Then you can decide that everything joint will be equally each of yours or that joint titling of property will only make the ownership proportionate to the contributions of each.

Whatever your intention, be careful to specify that with every new account or asset, since otherwise the presumption in law is usually that jointly owned property is equally owned. One of the issues unique to cohabiters is the issue of debt. That can lead to problems if one person's credit card is used to do the "heavy lifting" for furniture and appliances and the other party suddenly wants out. Without clarity between you, one could walk away with all the furniture and the other with all the debt!

Softening the Endings

While it is hard to end a relationship, at least the definition of when a living-together relationship is over is easy: you can agree that it is over when either sends a note to the other that the relationship is terminated. Then the provisions of your agreement as to asset division, housing arrangements, and so on will kick in.

There are additional things you can agree to do with and for each other, such as transitional support for the less wealthy or less well-employed partner if and when there is a breakup, so that person can ease out and into the next chapter of his or her life.

Till Death Do Us Part

That's the traditional wording in a marriage ceremony. And marriage confers certain rights to inheritance that do not automatically come with a living-together arrangement. That's why you can and should also provide for estate planning. In a living-together relationship, you cannot presume or assume anything, except that legal title rules. What you want to have pass to the other person must be in joint names or clearly gifted to the other, or the other must be designated as a beneficiary, as on life insurance policies and retirement assets.

Many bereaved lovers have watched incredulously as what they thought was their home was taken over by their lover's "rightful" heirs and the furniture emptied out only hours after the funeral of the beloved. Without clear titles to accompany an agreement, even an agreement may not be enough. Litigation can be avoided with correct titles on all the assets, so the legal protections are worth giving to and getting from each other.

BACK TO THE BEGINNINGS OF AGREEMENTS

The rules of the living-together agreements road are similar to those of a prenuptial agreement. You each need to have separate counsel, and you each need to make full disclosure of your assets and liabilities. The two of you need to understand the approach to conups of the jurisdiction in which you reside. Your road to reaching an agreement can then be guided by the rest of this book.

Even with a contract, there are certain rights—like Social Security benefits, hospital visitation by "closest relative," tax-free estate distributions, and others—that you may not be able to provide for each other. On a more positive note, with creative and careful planning, there are many mutual protections you can accomplish.

With creative and careful planning, there are many mutual protections you can accomplish.

You can draft a living will and a health-care power of attorney, giving your loved one the decision-making choices and giving you access to him or her in the hospital, even though you are not technically related. Depending on which state you live in, you may be able to enter into a civil union or form a domestic partnership. You can always employ the old legal workhorse of a power of attorney for limited purposes and for limited amounts of time. What you do *not* want to do is leave yourself or your beloved unprotected.

In reviewing various living-together contracts, or conup forms, you will see that they appear to anticipate more fundamental fairness between the parties than do the average prenuptial forms. One easy answer to the "why" of this is that typically, many people living together are both employed and each expects to continue to be so and to be an equal financial contributor.

The truth may be more complex. It may be that two people, who feel freed from the responsibilities of marriage but also denied its benefits, find themselves more protective of each other and understand that they share a common interest in fairness. There is a lesson in that for all of us as we contemplate the New Love Deal.

TOP COHABITATION DEAL ISSUES

Day-to-Day Issues:

- How will you handle daily living expenses, bank accounts, bill payments?

- How will you handle housing arrangements, title of property, mortgage payments?

- Does one party "buy in" to existing assets, such as a home you will share?

- If renting, whose name is on the rental agreement, and who will pay the rent if you separate? Can you afford it on your own?

- Who takes what property in the event of separation?

- How will your decisions impact the credit history of each person?

Longer-Term Considerations:

- Health-care power of attorney, living will instructions, estate plan

- Issues revolving around care and custody of children together, or from a previous marriage

- Documentation of ownership of gifts

- Life insurance ownership and beneficiary (note: the policy owner can change the beneficiary at any time)

- Retirement plan beneficiary (note: in the event of a split, there is no guaranteed retirement benefit to a cohabitant, and the owner can change the beneficiary)

Do you really want to be arguing about the above issues if your relationship doesn't survive? Isn't it better to be prepared with a written agreement, in advance, before the balance of power changes as you build a life together? You can see that it may look "easier" to just live together—but the financial, as well as emotional, consequences of a split can be just as devastating as if you were legally married.

Chapter 4:

NEW DEAL --SAME-SEX MARRIAGE AND/OR CIVIL UNIONS

Clearly we are a society in transition about relationships—what they stand for, what they mean, how long they should last, who should be in them, and who or what should govern them. The old answers were relatively easy. Marriage was between a man and a woman, it should last forever, government governed the marriage, and religion watched over it. Overall, those expectations were exactly what the Defense of Marriage Act (DOMA) was intended to reflect.

FEDERAL LAWS VERSUS STATE LAWS

How fast those traditional ideals are changing can be seen by the fact that DOMA itself was passed as recently as 1996, but the Supreme Court opined that it was in part unconstitutional in 2013. In mid-2013, a certain section of DOMA, namely §3, was declared unconstitutional. That part of the act had prevented federal law from extending federal benefits or programs to gay or lesbian couples, even if they were legally married in their own state of residence.

The case that brought attention to this issue is one in which a same-sex widow in New York was charged over $300,000 in inheritance taxes when her spouse died. She challenged DOMA because same-sex couples were not allowed the tax exemption that other married couples would get in New York, thereby denying her both her due process and equal protection rights under our Constitution, she claimed. The Supreme Court agreed with her in the landmark case *US v. Windsor.*

What makes this all so difficult is that § 2 of DOMA still is unchallenged, allowing states to deny recognition of the same-sex marriages that were entered into in another state that did allow them. So, in short, the federal government has to recognize and effectuate numerous federal spousal benefits to same-sex couples, but individual states do not.

Federal spousal rights are very significant and worth fighting for. They include Social Security benefits, health insurance and pensions for federal employee spouses, joint tax filing, benefits for military spouses, and myriad other potential gains, more of which we describe in the gay marriage section in this chapter.

Various courts were asked to rule on the issue of same-sex marriage during 2013, and late in the year a federal judge struck down Utah's ban on same-sex marriage, saying it conflicted with the constitutional guarantees of equal protection and due process. That ruling is being appealed as of this writing.

Then, in early 2014, Attorney General Eric Holder announced that the Obama administration would expand recognition of same-sex marriages in federal legal matters, including bankruptcies, prison visits, survivor benefits, and even the legal right for a spouse to refuse to testify to incriminate a spouse. Even in the thirty-four states that do not recognize same-sex marriages, those benefits will be extended to the extent that the federal government has jurisdiction. That means if a marriage takes place in a state that recognizes same-sex marriage, federal laws will recognize that marriage in any state the couple chooses to reside. So a couple married in Massachusetts, for example, where same-sex marriage is legal, could file as a couple for federal bankruptcy protection in a state that does not recognize their marriage for purposes of state law.

The relationship revolution is still ongoing and even accelerating. That's why you'll find continual updates to this chapter at our website, www.TheNewLoveDeal.com.

WHAT IS THE DEAL WITH CIVIL UNIONS?

Civil unions are just one option on the menu of New Love Deals. Modern families include permutations plus possibilities never imagined even a few years ago. They are our new realities. And the law is constantly evolving in an attempt to create legal order out of relationship chaos!

And the law is constantly evolving in an attempt to create legal order out of relationship chaos!

Illinois, for example, legalized same-sex marriage in late 2013. Before that, since 2011, gay couples had been able to enter into civil unions with their partners. Somewhat uniquely, Illinois law allowed both same-sex and opposite-sex couples to choose civil unions. Clearly, some couples will still opt for civil unions, despite the legalization of gay marriage.

Civil union couples can be treated like traditional spouses in many rights that really matter: they can make life-and-death medical decisions for each other, inherit from each other, and divorce each other. While the right to divorce can seem like the least appealing of benefits, it may be the most meaningful. It's hard to feel safe in a relationship that has no clear rules of property ownership or "rules of the road" should a breakup occur.

In a civil union, almost all the protections that marriage offers are present; it's the "almost" that will make this law more challenging. Civil unions provide a status equal to marriage but clearly separate from it. We all remember how complicated and unsatisfactory anything "separate but equal" can turn out to be. Since this legal status is so new, its legal pros and cons are still being evaluated.

RELATIONSHIP DEALS IN EVOLUTION

The new answers on relationships are now complex and further complicated by the autonomy of each state under our federal government, and the unclear interaction of federal and state laws. This chapter of "relationship deals" has yet to be finally written by the legislature or courts. Therefore, your authors cannot really write the final word on how to view civil unions, except to say proceed with caution—and check www.TheNewLoveDeal.com for updates.

Still another interesting question about civil unions is what effect they will have on cohabiting couples and public policy overall, since there is an increasing preference for living together without benefit of marriage.

Because we are based here, Illinois problems are easy ones for us to highlight. For years, the state's public policy was traditional in every sense of the word. Even if unmarried couples tried to make legal arrangements to protect each other, the courts frowned on them; judges scrutinized them, and often denied their enforceability, especially if anything about the sexual nature of the relationship was even implied.

Other states actually have been more accepting of cohabitation agreements and contracts for unmarried couples. Since an easy definition of a civil union is a committed relationship, but not quite as committed as a marriage, acceptance of civil unions seems to signal a new openness to alternative lifestyles, whether by same-sex or heterosexual couples.

Eight states, besides Illinois, currently recognize civil unions. They are: Colorado, Connecticut, Delaware, Hawaii, New Hampshire, New Jersey, Rhode Island, and Vermont. In addition, legal domestic partnerships (similar to civil unions) are recognized in several other states. And as the growing legalization of same-sex marriage crosses the country, there will be plenty of changes in the law. Cohabitation agreements will receive different recognition, depending on the state of residence, no matter what the sexual orientation of the couple.

TAMING TRANSITIONS AND UNCERTAINTY

What is clear is that those in gay marriages and civil unions are going to need written agreements to supplement and secure their financial understandings until and unless gay marriage becomes the law of the land in each and every state, as well as at the federal level. That is a legal battle that may wage for a long while, and the uncertainty is unsettled and unsettling.

Not every state recognizes gay marriages or civil unions; however, couples of all persuasions move around freely in these free United States, which in turn complicates their legal status. The extension of federal rights seemingly does not yet apply to civil unions even in states where civil unions are legal. That, like everything in this area of the law, may or may not change.

The law is unpredictable, with sometimes one step forward becoming two steps back—or at least sideways. Hawaii, for example, was set to have gay marriage after its supreme court ruled in favor of it, but then backpedaled, and its state legislature has not moved forward to legalize same-sex marriages.

As long as our societal norms are in flux, the law regarding property rights will remain in flux and unpredictable.

More Confusion

In case the laws have not created sufficient confusion, there are a couple of other significant factors to be considered. The law is not clear as to what state will govern the divorces of gay couples and what the "portability" is of your various rights. Therefore, if a legally married same-sex couple moves to a state that does not recognize gay marriage, even their federal benefits may be in jeopardy, or at least very much harder to achieve, and they may not even be able to divorce where they actually live.

Before a couple of any persuasion or commitment level decides to move from one state to another, it is important to consider the legal effects of the move, which means you must consult knowledgeable attorney(s) in the state of your destination. Believe it or not, even the traditionally married need to double-check the law of the destination state because traditional family law and its application also varies from state to state. For gay couples or the civilly unionized, the risk escalates exponentially.

SOME DEAL ISSUES UNIQUE TO GAY MARRIAGES

Our country is now divided not just into north and south, or red states and blue states, but also into the sixteen states (including DC) that recognize marriage equality, the thirty-five states that prohibit gay marriage, and any of the citizens in all the states that disagree with their state policy.

Oddly, and at least for now, the federal government is (mostly) aligned with both groups as to the granting or the denial of federal benefits and will defer to the individual states. If you think this is an unpredictable and volatile set of circumstances, you are entirely right.

If your wedding was celebrated in a state that recognizes marital equality, your federal bread basket of rights has just been expanded in "let me count (some of) the ways":

- Social security, but be sure to check with your state's law

- Employer health insurance

- ERISA rights

- All kinds of tax-related benefits—from filing jointly, to divorcing "equally," to estate planning jointly—but check with your experts

- Visas for your foreign spouse

- Life insurance

- Adoption—mostly

- Bankruptcy

- Premarital contracts

- Custody

WHY YOU NEED TO MAKE YOUR OWN DEAL

The intolerable confusion and changing landscape of gay rights is perhaps the single best argument to be made for premarital agreements. It is possible that the agreement may be recognized even if and where your relationship is not; at the very least, it can allocate your rights, set forth your agreements, and unequivocally express your intentions.

Bottom line: if you are in any long-term relationship, a written contract regarding your rights and expectations is a necessary "safety plan." It can help protect you if you move—or if the law moves. And as the relationship world turns, traditional marriages will increasingly benefit from spouses writing their own deals along with their own vows.

SAME-SEX RELATIONSHIP CHOICES

If you are a same-sex couple trying to build permanence into your relationship, you now have a wider variety of options. However, as noted above, the relationship you choose may not be legally respected in all states. That's why it's so important to do some planning, whether you just choose to live together or to find a way to legalize your relationship. The first step is to get legal help in your state of residence to learn your options, among the following:

Traditional marriage

Gay marriage

Cohabitation agreement

Civil union

Domestic partnership

No matter which one of these options you choose, you need to be aware of the interaction of state and federal law when planning for your future. And in most cases, you are wise to supplement your relationship with a written agreement, planning for these contingencies. All a layperson really needs to know for sure is that you must check with an accountant and an attorney when planning your future, because your legal domicile will affect your legal destiny.

Chapter 5:

A Judge's View of Sharing

You might wonder what I am thinking when I am sitting on the bench in my black robe, gavel at the ready, about to rule on your petition for dissolution, support, or child custody. Likely, I am wondering where you started out and whether you ever considered it might end like this.

Not surprisingly, we judges often discover that these conflicts are propelled more by emotions than by law. By the time people find themselves in that dark, inhospitable place called divorce court, they have lost their ability to understand how they arrived at such a place.

In my career as a judge, I presided over thousands of divorce cases, and I also have performed hundreds of marriage ceremonies! Earlier, as an attorney, I wrote prenuptial, cohabitation, and civil union agreements—as well as providing counseling for couples joining their lives. In the world of marriage and relationships, I have done everything but deliver the babies. From these experiences, I have learned that disastrous consequences often result when people have disregarded or failed to communicate their needs.

The impact of that truth was never as clear to me as when my friend Jim described his experience in his divorce trial (not in my court). He moaned: "Yesterday in court, standing across the room was Sandy, who had not only been my love, but my confidant and friend. Yet there she sat, with her lawyer literally blockading me from speaking to her. Could this angry and hostile woman really be the same person I married? I always thought we could talk about everything, but we never really discussed money. And now that's all she wants to talk about!"

Neglected conversations about how money would be divided haunt many of my cases. Curiously, I see couples in my courtroom desperately trying to unravel the chaos of their current lives, expecting heightened communication to occur at the end of the relationship or marriage. Too often, sadly, they were unwilling to have this same degree and quality of communication during the pre-living-together or premarital stage. These couples often erroneously expect that their conflict about essential matters will be easier to handle during difficult times, when communication is managed through lawyers.

As I have watched these couples suffer a bombardment of frustration, betrayal, and anger, I have realized how much better things would have been had there been open and revealing communication in the beginning of their relationship. If only they had learned to negotiate potential conflict and not shy away from uncomfortable issues, things might have ended differently. Many subjects, like finances, time with the children of the marriage, and lifestyle priorities, including vacations and the participation of the in-laws in their lives, could have been far less stressful if they had been addressed in advance.

I have realized after years of experience as an attorney and judge that many couples don't communicate early on enough about what they need from their relationship or what their expectations are from their mate. I now believe that cohabitation, civil union, or pre-nuptial agreements provide one of the most remarkable opportunities for couples to learn how to navigate the turbulent waters of potentially perilous topics.

You're about to take a big step, whether it's marriage or a long-term commitment to live together. Make sure you start off in the right direction.

In this chapter and the next, you'll learn the techniques of sharing your innermost feelings and thoughts, and the eight critical needs that must be addressed if your relationship is to survive for the long term. If you can't share emotionally, there is little chance that the lawyers can create an agreement that will keep your marriage intact. And then, if you're willing to dig a little deeper, you'll be interested in seeing the basic needs of your partner that must be met in order to make your relationship one of the unions that lasts for a lifetime.

If you can't share emotionally, there is little chance that the lawyers can create an agreement that will keep your marriage intact.

How do I know? Because I have a front- row seat at watching marriages dissolve. Many of those marriages break up over issues that could have been resolved if only the partners had understood these basic concepts and needs. So first, here are five important steps to making your relationship work. If you get this part right, drafting your agreement will be a far easier.

STEP 1: COMMUNICATE

Most of us have not acquired a flexible enough vocabulary for getting our deepest needs met. To get our own needs met, we must know ourselves and have a genuine awareness of our true expectations. When we know what we need and when we can share those intimacies, we have taken the initial step toward real and transforming communication. That skill will serve us well throughout the relationship or marriage.

You wouldn't start a game without knowing the rules, nor should you start negotiating a cohabitation or prenuptial agreement without understanding the unifying and often conflicting needs of your partner. And to have a successful outcome, you need to learn how to truly listen to your partner. Forgive me a moment for getting off the legalities of marriage and into the areas where, from experience on the bench, I know that marriages fail. The critical missing ingredient is almost always communication.

As you begin communicating about the agreement, allow your mate to completely exhaust any fears concerning the process and resulting agreement. Each of you should feel free to explain why you think a cohabitation, civil union, or prenuptial agreement will, or will not, be beneficial. Try not to react or formulate a response until your partner is finished, so that when you do respond, it gives the impression that you are trying to understand his or her position. This will not be easy, as this conversation is almost always about trust.

STEP 2: SOLIDIFY TRUST

The long-term benefit to a relationship or marriage is that couples who have learned how to listen to each other have created safety zones where they can reveal parts of themselves and what they truly want. The more you reveal yourself, and the more you are accepted by your mate, the more you solidify trust.

That kind of trust is the basis for a prenuptial agreement, for a successful relationship, for solving the inevitable problems that will arise—and even for dealing with attorneys, if the relationship terminates. Once you become opponents in court, trust disappears. Before you get to that point, where you are sitting on the hard wooden benches of my divorce court, listening to the lawyers argue blame and fault, you need to define and treasure your zone of trusted communication. Only when you base this conversation on trust can it be productive.

STEP 3: LEARN HOW TO LISTEN

As an attorney and judge, I have learned how valuable real listening skills are. I would like to share some of this information with you, as I realize that truly hearing someone during these difficult conversations is challenging. So, here are some important considerations when you meet this challenge.

The greater the emotional extreme, the less people hear, regardless of the emotion. It is futile to attempt to reason with an angry person.

Allow a partner to finish speaking and then ask if she or he has anything else to add. If you speak before the other is finished, your words will be automatically filtered out. Fifty-one percent of the human brain is dedicated to visual referencing, so how you appear to listen—with your body language, eye contact, and posture—counts very much.

Whoever asks the questions controls the communication. Try to ask open-ended questions, such as, "What happened next?" Don't use the word *why* because it makes people psychologically defensive. Instead of *why,* ask: "What factors brought you to that decision?"

When your partner is angry, help him or her feel safe and willing to continue to share with you. The time when people are the most emotional or angry is the time for you to become the most alert and curious. The more furious they are, the more curious you should be. Do not respond in kind, but ask yourself what is really behind their reaction. If you don't understand the source of their feelings, you will end up experiencing only the effects of their feelings.

> *If you don't understand the source of their feelings, you will end up experiencing only the effects of their feelings.*

The reality is that when people feel safe, they will listen to almost anything—especially if they trust your motives. If your partner believes that you are trying to push her or him into something for your own exclusive benefit, or into a settlement that she or he doesn't feel comfortable with, your partner will quickly tune you out.

STEP 4: BE AWARE OF FEEDBACK; RESPOND REASONABLY

Be aware of feedback from your partner. Recognize the moment when the conversation starts to become intense. That is when your partner is starting to feel unsafe. How do you react? Check your own heart rate. Is there increased gesturing, rising voices, or finger-pointing? Is either of you becoming withdrawn or going into fear mode? We react to threats with either fight or flight. Neither reaction brings about a constructive agreement.

The last thing you want to do, when your partner begins feeling unsafe and subsequently attacks, is mimic his or her behavior. Keep your ego out of it. Know that you are not actually being attacked. It's just that your partner is feeling anxious, unsafe, and defensive.

When your partner is reluctant to open up, try using a mirroring technique. Guess at the source of the anger from the clues that you have. For example, try probing with, "While you are saying one thing, I think you are actually angry, which I sense from your tone or expression." This has to be done in your most even tone of voice to remodel what is going on. Then paraphrase what you think he or she might say. For example, "While you say nothing is wrong, I think you are upset that we are talking about this topic."

If your partner remains unresponsive, don't push too hard. Instead, ask what she or he would like your next step to be. This moves your partner's brain from emotional to problem-solving mode.

Step 5: Manage Agreement

What if you disagree with him or her? First, pick out the parts where you agree, so you don't end up arguing over a fine point and forget about how much you do agree upon. We are all trained to scan for minor points of disagreement. Identifying them allows us to feel smart and right. Skilled negotiators emphasize the points of agreement and build from them. If you completely disagree, you might suggest: "I think I see things differently. May I describe how?"

By now, you recognize that these techniques are not only useful in considering a prenuptial agreement or a living-together contract; they are the basis for open communication, which is what allows any relationship to succeed. Use the checklist at the end of this chapter to start the process of sharing, communicating, and listening with your love.

CONVERSATIONAL WARM-UPS

Suggestion: Review the following conversational warm-up list alone, with a pen and paper, weighing each item on the list privately prior to reviewing it with the spouse-to-be. Wait a day to reconsider your initial answers to see if they change on the second reading. Only then should you move on to the specific discussion points in chapter 6.

Rank the following statements from one to ten based on how strongly you agree with them, ten being the most, one being the least:

- It is important to me to feel trusted.

- Talking about the possibilities for breakup or divorce remind me of my last breakup.

- I am still very much affected by my last breakup or divorce.

- I am angry when I do not feel trusted.

- I am sad when I do not feel trusted.

- It is important for me to share the joy of financial success with my partner.

- I believe that financial generosity is a sign of love.

- If my partner loves me now, he or she should still care about my welfare even if we are not together.

- I believe that my partner is the most important person in the world.

A Judge's View of "Needs"

Once you are in front of me in divorce court, I can only rule on the issues presented to me. I often regret that the two people—and their expensive attorneys—who are standing in front of me pleading their case did not know how important it was to communicate with each other and understand each other's needs before things reached this point.

So, from up here on the bench, let me point out my conclusions about eight critical needs that must be addressed—not only to negotiate a prenuptial or cohabitation agreement, but to ensure that it will never be triggered!

Think carefully about how you and your partner react to and value each other's basic needs. If you cannot discuss them, respect them even if you disagree with some of them, and accommodate them, then all the carefully crafted legal agreements will not keep your relationship together. You will see each other in court.

THE NEED TO HAVE SIMILAR CORE VALUES

When you and your partner share your financial values (for example, intended contributions to charity, what sums of money to give your children, and ideas about retirement), you each gain insight into what core values your partner brings to the marriage. You may also discover how the other person envisions making these things happen. If you uncover a basic disparity in core values, your relationship is starting out with a huge strain. These are issues you may never be willing to compromise, or able to change about yourself or your partner. But the best chance of reaching a compromise occurs while you are bathing in a sea of romantic love.

The long-term benefit to the relationship or marriage is that you will know where you agree and where you don't, so that you will not feel ambushed in the future over an issue involving different values. If you discover later in the game that your values are different, you may feel resentful when these differences are first revealed, as if a secret had been kept from you. Whatever you're afraid to talk about—whether the relationship with children from a previous marriage, or issues about saving and spending, or your true beliefs about marital fidelity—now is the time to state your core values. Better to find out sooner than later.

THE NEED TO BE ACCEPTED WITH OUR SCARS AND IMPERFECTIONS

Yes, we all have scars and imperfections. Yet revealing them is one of the reasons that prenuptial agreements can be frightening. Scars and imperfections are often generated from past personal experiences. They may be based on a bad divorce, guilt about children from a former marriage, or perhaps dependency on one's parents. We admit fragility when it becomes clear that we want to be protected from further pain after a bad breakup or divorce. Some of the topics that tend to reveal our flaws remind our partner that we are not totally fresh and innocent—and we so much want to look our best to the one we love.

The long-term benefit of a cohabitation, civil union, or prenuptial agreement is that there will no longer be hidden agendas or confusion about behavior in our mate. We will come to understand the unique behavior of our partner, as we observe this person we love trying to protect her- or himself from discomfort or pain. Understanding and acceptance from our partner is the ultimate form of intimacy.

THE NEED FOR TRUST

A cohabitation, civil union, or prenuptial agreement is often taken to be an inference of lack of trust by the party with fewer assets; however, it is an ultimate act of building trust when you ask your partner for financial protections while still maintaining the affection between you.

It may follow like this: "I have asked you for a prenuptial agreement. We have negotiated, and even have had some ugly moments, but I still trust you not to hold these moments against us, and I trust that at the end of these negotiations, we will be even closer."

The long-term value to the relationship or marriage of addressing this need is immense. You learn that trust is not lost just because there is conflict or differences of opinion, or even because you have both experienced painful moments.

Trust is not lost just because there is conflict or differences of opinion

THE NEED TO FEEL FINANCIALLY SECURE

Fears about the scarcity of money can be based more on a state of mind than on reality. These fears may originate in early childhood or have been formed as a result of a bad divorce. Discussions might include each revealing what happened in his or her last relationship or divorce, or some previous financial difficulties, which makes him or her especially fearful of being without money.

The long-term value to the relationship is that discussing your emotional orientation toward money prevents a distorted perception about each other's motives. Words such as cheap, selfish, and opportunistic can be eliminated. When your spouse acts irrationally (in your opinion) about finances, there doesn't have to be a negative inference, nor do you have to take it personally.

THE NEED FOR BALANCE

This need is particularly complicated when creating an agreement where assets are uneven or family wealth is involved. Suddenly, the partner with fewer assets is negotiating with not only a lover, but the parents, who may remain in the shadows, while really pulling the strings. That kind of influence can be devastating and unbalancing to the relationship, and to future relations with in-laws, if not discussed openly.

One of the most frequent reasons couples turn against each other is as a result of what I call "shadowboxing." That's what happens when there is a breakdown of communication between a husband and wife who are no longer talking only to each other. They are also trying to negotiate with people who are not in the room but rather in the shadows. In my courtroom, I call these people UFOs: unidentified family obstructionists.

Maneuvering these loyalties can be inflammatory when it is structured as a "love test." The no-win positioning of a love test requires the partner with the assets to "choose" to whom he or she is more loyal: his or her life mate, parents, or children from a prior relationship or marriage.

The long-term value to the relationship or marriage of having these discussions prior to living together or marrying is immeasurable. Each party then understands in advance that problems with relatives may occur in the future. Prior to the problems occurring, the parties can better allocate their mutual time and financial loyalties—for example, deciding on what time will be spent with the children from a prior relationship or marriage, or which holidays will be spent with which in-laws.

There is a tremendous advantage to having these discussions early on, before the parties have been repeatedly offended during the relationship or marriage by their partner's choice of loyalties, and have therefore lost their objectivity.

THE NEED FOR APPRECIATION

Very often, the partner who has fewer assets has not been a witness to the work and struggles of the partner-to-be. The one with fewer assets has not seen what his or her future spouse went through to accumulate them, so those efforts may be overlooked when negotiating the prenuptial agreement. The partner-to-be with the greater assets, who is now in a position to share that wealth with someone he or she loves, is unsure that he or she wants to share those assets in the event he or she is not with that person.

The long-term value to the relationship or marriage of discussing these issues early on is that the spouse with fewer assets may acknowledge the premarital hard work of the other spouse. The one who has earned the money is relieved to know her or his partner appreciates her or his efforts, rather than taking them for granted. And, in the process, the one who has fewer assets understands that she or he is valued in a different and more important way than mere financial assets.

THE NEED FOR MUTUAL VULNERABILITY

The very core of intimacy is mutual vulnerability. Often, cohabitation, civil union, or prenuptial agreements shift the financial risk of marital failure to one of the parties. In those cases, shifting the financial risk actually shifts the balance of power in the parties' relationship as well.

The very core of intimacy is mutual vulnerability

For example, if the agreement does not provide adequately for the partner's future in the event of a breakup or divorce, conflict during the relationship or marriage may have dangerous consequences. One spouse might have to appease the other for fear of suffering the negative financial consequences contained in the prenuptial agreement. In a state of constant appeasement, that person will not be able to ask for what he or she really needs, and before long, he or she may conform to a template of behavior that is not authentic and is destined to breed resentment. The spouse with the financial upper hand may never feel the need to compromise, but instead become even more domineering.

It is the act of compromising that makes couples evolve and become closer. The long-term value to the relationship of participating in these negotiations is that the parties understand why mutual vulnerability is important. An unfair document heavily shifting the balance of power to one of the parties can be a silent killer.

THE NEED TO SHARE

If the partner with less financial worth is not given any benefit for an increase in prerelationship or nonmarital assets, she or he may be excluded from the excitement and joy when there is good fortune. Eventually, the party with more assets might learn not to share successes with her or his spouse, as it becomes a topic of conflict. If there are decisions to be made about the prerelationship or nonmarital assets, chances are the partner with less may not be consulted at all, thereby disregarding her or his need to share in a partner's joy.

The long-term value to the relationship or marriage of these discussions is that the party with the assets will realize how alienating it is for a partner to be separated from the other's financial success. Suggestions on how to handle this will be discussed in other chapters, but suffice it to say that unless there is some small participation, those prerelationship or nonmarital assets can become viewed as the "other woman/man." The assets may become a topic of secrecy, not discussed, and a breeding ground for resentment. In retaliation, the excluded partner might become secretive about other things, resulting in each party's building bridges away from open communication.

NOW, YOU'RE READY TO START

By going through each one of the needs with a partner-to-be, both of you will have elegantly opened up the discussions. By using the topic warm-ups at the end of this chapter, you will have a pathway to communication about relationship issues that is less personal and more universal. That should make communications even easier. Each statement on the list is associated with one of the needs referred to in this chapter. Couples might find it helpful to refer back to that specific basic need as they discuss the items on the list.

Every time one of these conversations is resolved, with the inevitable better understanding of each other, congratulations are in order. The couple is well on the way toward reaching the pinnacle of that unspoken intimate zone of successfully mixing love, finances, and future expectations. That's a true accomplishment.

TOPICS FOR AN INTIMATE CONVERSATION ABOUT NEEDS

Suggestion: Partners should try to avoid giving feedback until the other person has finished speaking, and remember that they do not have to deal with every issue in one conversation. In fact, if they try to, it will probably exhaust them, and may prove counterproductive. Finally, when finished with this exercise, couples should acknowledge their mate for trusting them and revealing intimate feelings, and then agree on a date and time to continue the discussion.

- It is important that I am not taken for granted financially.

- It is important that I do not feel exploited financially.

- I am worried that I will be financially disadvantaged if this marriage does not last.

- I am worried that my children will be financially disadvantaged if this marriage does not last or if I die before my spouse.

- I am worried about alienating my initial family.

- I worry about my obligations to my initial family.

- Protecting my initial family is very important to me.

- It is important for me to have my parents comfortable with our agreement.

- Trust means never keeping things private from your spouse.

- I can trust my partner and at the same time protect myself.

- I will not hold my partner responsible for my bad experiences in my last relationship.

- It bothers me when I think my partner does not understand me.

- I really should give up my beliefs so my mate will not be angry with me.

- Protecting my mate if anything should happen to me is very important to me.

- Negotiating these agreements is very difficult for me.

- I am not used to asking for what I need in a love relationship.

- I am not used to getting what I need in a love relationship.

- It is important for me to keep my financial independence.

- Guilt plays a big part in my relationships.

- If I hurt someone's feelings, it is very important for me to make it right as soon as possible.

- I am willing to take risks beyond my comfort zone to make a better relationship.

- I am willing to be vulnerable and dependent upon my mate.

Chapter 7:

THE BOTTOM LINE: LOVE AND MONEY

When it comes to money, there are basically two types of people: Savers and Spenders. And for better or worse, they tend to love each other! When that happens, you've created the potential for huge problems in your relationship. You cannot simply "command" your partner to agree with your inherent money style. So if you're going

You cannot simply "command" your partner to agree with your inherent money style.

to live happily ever after, you will each need to make adjustments—and understand the financial "deal-breakers" in your personalities.

This chapter is not about changing your money style. By the time you're a consenting adult and ready for marriage or an extended commitment to live together, your beliefs and attitudes are well entrenched. It's about recognizing that those unconscious tendencies may well grate upon your partner, who was raised to have an entirely different approach to money matters.

No matter what your money personality type or your financial status, it is certainly possible to build a loving, honest, and long-lasting marriage or relationship. It just won't happen by accident. Since you can't change each other's ingrained beliefs, it's important to acknowledge and respect those differences.

It's equally important to come up with a framework that will allow you to deal with inevitable differences when they arise. Financial planning and agreement in advance of marriage or living together is the only way to minimize conflicts that could undermine your life together. And it could help you avoid some unpleasant surprises if your relationship does not work out.

Joanie, who was married to a spendthrift husband, thought his excessive spending was romantic while they were dating, troublesome after they were married, and actually tragic when they were divorcing. All those flat-screen TVs and extravagant electronic toys had been delivered to the house and paid for with joint credit cards. So, the astronomical debt belonged to both of them.

At the opposite end of the spectrum, Bill inherited $2 million and did not think twice about putting it in a joint account "because we love each other." During his divorce two years later, he found he had unintentionally "made a gift" of $2 million to a failing marriage when he deposited the money into a jointly owned account. Now, according to his state's law, half was hers!

Susan and Jane had a civil union and also had two children together. Their state did not allow same-sex marriages. Susan had a high-paying job, a pension, and an IRA, while Jane decided to be a more "traditional" mom and stay home with the kids. Susan's retirement plan would have to cover them both, since Jane couldn't contribute to an IRA, unlike a legally married nonworking spouse. What would happen if they split up down the road? Absent a legal marriage, Jane has no spousal right to her partner's retirement assets.

George and Sharon have been living together for years. In fact, everyone thinks they're married. But if George dies, Sharon will not be able to collect on his Social Security benefits as a widow. Did she remember to ask him to purchase life insurance, naming her as a beneficiary, to make up for this limitation?

These are the kinds of "surprises" that can be avoided with some creative planning and a prenuptial or cohabitation agreement. By the way, the agreement does not mean that you cannot and should not be just and generous to each other. It simply means that everyone is making conscious choices and informed decisions.

MONEY AS POWER

In a relationship, money has two vastly different aspects—the specifics of money management, and the unspoken dynamic of money as power. When we talk about "money differences," you're probably thinking about specifics—the kind of financial decisions that you and your spouse or partner are likely to make together or argue about. These are the kind of decisions that could cause serious disagreements, such as:

Money has two vastly different aspects—the specifics of money management, and the unspoken dynamic of money as power.

- Should we take a vacation or save for a house?

- Should we buy a sports car or a family sedan?

- Should we risk moving for a new job and promotion?

- Should we go into debt to remodel the kitchen?

- Can we afford to send the kids to summer camp, or take a vacation?

You would think that two rational adults could discuss these money issues and come to a reasonable compromise. But those daily life decisions may be just the tip of the iceberg. They reveal the basic differences in how we think about, and prioritize, spending, saving, and investing money. But they may also reveal a subtle dynamic of power in the relationship. All too often, financial issues that should be solved over the kitchen table turn into heated arguments that move to the bedroom—and all the chambers of your heart.

THE MONEY BATTLEGROUND

Too frequently, money matters morph into issues of power and control. That's when you encounter the real money issues—the power trip that gives one party a feeling of control over the other, and corresponding feelings of resentment from the one who feels controlled. The specifics of saving or spending

Too frequently, money matters morph into issues of power and control

become a backdrop to a different kind of struggle for dominance in the relationship.

My best advice is: *don't let money become a battleground!*

The only way to avoid those battles is to understand each other's money personalities and then to set up systems for making money decisions that respect each person's desires and values. Those arrangements must work regardless of who earns more money—or even if one spouse earns all the money. Read on, for specifics of setting up these systems.

If a marriage or relationship is to be equally balanced between two loving partners, there cannot be inequality in the financial arrangements because of a perceived financial "power" of one party over the other. You may choose to agree that one spouse will take over certain financial chores, and you may acknowledge that one spouse has more experience, or interest, in certain financial and investment decisions. But if one of you cedes *all* the financial decision making to the other merely to avoid an argument or stress, then you've increased the odds of future failure.

MONEY AND EMOTIONS

Talking about money in the context of a loving relationship is troubling to many people. But it's a critical part of the New Love Deal. And if you decide to avoid this chapter entirely, you're tempting fate. It's not just about financial planning; it's about the emotional volatility that money decisions engender.

No one is immune from those two most basic emotions: *fear and greed.*

Whenever you make a significant money decision, those two emotions are likely to arise in one or both of you. And your visceral responses might be quite different. It's hard to explain that rush of emotion that immediately creates a reaction—to take a risk or to avoid it completely. Emotions supersede rational thought, often with devastating financial consequences.

Think of all the people who fall for "too good to be true" scams. Once exposed, the scams seem so obvious. But greed blinds people to the obvious. Those irrational emotions impact even the small decisions we make on a daily basis—unless we are conscious of their existence and force ourselves to think rationally. You can exercise that discipline over yourself—but it is difficult to make your partner aware of how his or her most innate emotions impact decision making.

MONEY PERSONALITIES

Your "money personality" is something deep within, formulated in childhood—whether from genes or environment. And your emotional reaction to money is not something you can change in yourself, much less in your partner. The only way to handle it is to respect each other's money personality and to set up systems for dealing with the inevitable conflicts.

To respect each other's money personality and to set up systems for dealing with the inevitable conflicts.

Any personality contrasts are very obvious when the decision is about investing. You start talking about how to invest in your retirement plan at work, or consider a real estate investment at a "bargain" price, or want to put money into a great business venture.

Then, different perspectives appear instantly. One of you sees immediate dollar signs and starts dreaming about how you'll spend the profits—new car, vacation home, travel. The other sees money disappearing. What if the stock falls or the market crashes or the business fails? All that hard-earned money could be lost. Fear and greed intrude, sowing the seeds for conflict. No matter what the decision is, if it is made out of emotion, there will be recriminations later.

And recriminations are something to avoid at all costs. People make mistakes. Some are honest mistakes, some are emotional mistakes. But your marriage was *not* a mistake—and you cannot let your financial disagreements fester.

Disagreement is not inevitable—if you've created a formula for discussion and decisions, a road map based on your understanding of each other's money personalities. Conflict can be replaced by compromise. Perhaps a smaller sum could be invested. But if it's an all-or-none financial decision that is required, at least there will be a sensible forum for discussion. That's a basic requirement for dealing with money issues.

Emotional conflicts are obvious in the big-money decisions, but not so apparent in everyday life. One person insists on paying credit card bills in full every month, never incurring an interest charge. The other figures it's worth buying that bargain, even if it can't be paid off for a couple of months. One sees a romantic dinner at a candlelit restaurant as an "investment" in the relationship; the other sees it as money "down the drain."

It's important to recognize that while the conflicts are inevitable, there is no one right answer. It's up to you to decide as a couple. You may decide to keep some of or all your financial assets separate, lessening the need for conflict. But unless you realize that you're filing a joint tax return (or paying a significant tax penalty for filing separately if married), saving for a joint future, and living in a shared household, your efforts to lead separate financial lives are bound to fail. That's especially true in a community property state, where both assets and responsibilities are commingled by law.

A financial planner can create an investment plan based on your age, assets, and risk tolerance, using market history and economic models. Computer software can help you organize and track your spending and saving. A lawyer can explain the differences between documents required for a legal marriage, a civil union, or just an agreement to cohabit.

However, no outsider can create a structure that will mediate your everyday money decisions. Only you, as a couple, can do that. And the best time to do that kind of planning is when you're most optimistic about your future together.

That's why the New Love Deal is mostly about money.

THE "PRE-DEAL" MONEY TALK

If this book does nothing more than guide you through this essential financial discussion, it will have been worth the purchase price. And if you think your relationship can't take the risk of this kind of open, honest discussion about money, the price of the book will be far, far less expensive than the cost of a divorce!

Please note that this process of coming to agreement is not just about revealing assets or dividing income. Whether or not you decide to create a legal agreement, you need to have this talk about money well before you join your lives together.

The discussion starts with respect for each other—the most essential ingredient in any deal, but especially an arrangement of the heart. If you don't respect yourself—as well as your partner—all the money in the world won't make yours a happy relationship. Respect means acknowledging and valuing your partner's position, despite your own feelings of disagreement. Respect is the starting point for an honest discussion, and a successful resolution, be it a compromise or a complete acceptance of the other's position. Or it can result in an agreement to disagree about these issues and create plans for how you will handle those future disagreements!

Respect means acknowledging and valuing your partner's position, despite your own feelings of disagreement.

TACKLING MONEY DIFFERENCES

So, this is the point where you open the book with your prospective life partner and say: "Let's talk about money and follow this checklist." The only rule for this discussion is that it be done with complete honesty and mutual respect.

This is not a debate, though there will be inevitable differences. In fact, life together would be so boring if you agreed completely on all these money issues. But you can't build togetherness until you understand and acknowledge the power of your different money attitudes and habits. Plus, you'll be far more understanding of the reasons for your differences, whether they come from previous experiences, memories of your parents, or just your instinctive reactions.

One more thing: before you talk, remember that in life, timing is everything! This is a conversation that may last for days or weeks. You should schedule the starting point to take place when you're not stressed about wedding plans or calling the movers, worried about a specific money issue, or exhausted from work. Find a quiet, comfortable place to talk—and don't just spring it on your partner. (You'll find that's good advice for any discussion in your relationship.)

SIX STEPS TO GETTING STARTED

STEP 1: FIGURE OUT WHETHER YOU ARE A SAVER OR A SPENDER

Start by describing your own money personality. You may never have given it a thought and have taken your style for granted. But now your partner's wishes may challenge your own values. It's time to understand just who you are when it comes to money decisions. Remember, this is not a judgment; it's an evaluation. Some things to reveal about yourself:

- How do you know you are what you think you are— saver or spender?

- What are some examples that demonstrate your money style?

- Do you think you are an extreme spender or extreme saver, or do you just tilt moderately in one direction?

- Are you comfortable carrying debt, or do you insist on being debt-free?

- What did you learn about money from your parents— i.e., did you learn to be frugal and budget, or did your parents constantly argue about money—and how do those experiences impact your feelings about money and marriage?

- Are there circumstances that accentuate your style— e.g., do you get really worried around tax time, when you're facing an annual salary review, or at the holiday season?

- Are there better times for you to think about money and make decisions—e.g., in the morning or after dinner?

STEP 2: ASSESS YOUR RISK TOLERANCE

Of course, no one wants to lose hard-earned money. But people really do have different risk tolerances. The trader who spends all day making buy-and-sell decisions has a far different risk tolerance than the long-term investor. Maybe risk tolerance is in the genes, or perhaps it's learned at a young age. Maybe it's a function of knowledge and perspective. Maybe it changes as you assume more responsibilities—for example, family and children.

Talk about where you are now, remembering that you're about to assume the greatest risk of all: a committed relationship.

Your Risk Tolerance Checklist:

- Do you think you're a risk taker when it comes to money? When it comes to career? When it comes to love?

- What is the most difficult type of risk for you to take—financial or emotional?

- What role do you think your parents played in your ability to tolerate risk?

- What role have your previous life experiences played?

- Do you think that a discussion of risk and a respectful, persuasive argument for risk made by your partner could allay some of your fears in making a specific decision?

STEP 3: DETERMINE YOUR MONEY MANAGEMENT STYLE

This is not only a practical issue, but a serious one. Some people are true organizers. Their checkbooks are up-to-date, or they use online money management tools, and they file retirement plan and mutual fund statements conscientiously. That's my style, and I keep file boxes and secure online documentation to an extreme that some would find truly annoying. Others can't seem to find anything—last year's tax return, receipts for major expenditures, product instruction manuals (how does that oven self-clean?). I don't know how they get through life; it would drive me crazy.

And it might drive you crazy, too. Talk about it and become aware of your differences. These don't have to be deal-breakers. In fact, in the next section of this chapter, you'll find my recommendations for relationship harmony when it comes to money matters. The organizational issue is the easiest problem to fix!

Consider the questions below about your current money management style as a way to get the conversation started:

Your Money Management Style

- Are you organized, and does it matter to you whether your partner is organized? Test: If the house were on fire, could you grab one box or file along with those treasured family photos so you could reconstruct your financial life?

- Do you pay your bills the day they arrive, once a month, whenever you get around to it? Or have you set up auto-pay for regular bills?

- Do you track your balances, or just figure "it's okay as long as the check doesn't bounce"?

- Do you usually pay your credit card balance in full every month—or sometimes just the minimum?

- Do you review your investments at least twice a year—or just figure you'll open the annual statement and hope you've made money?

- Do you rely on experts—tax preparer, broker, financial advisor—or are you a do-it-yourself type of person when it comes to money management?

Okay, calm down. Remember, there are no right or wrong answers, only differing styles, which can cause daily conflict. But we can fix that! Now it's time to get into deeper issues, the ones that have the potential to derail your relationship.

STEP 4: CHECK YOUR CREDIT HISTORY

Now you're ready to share your past financial life. The easiest way to do it is to get your credit report online and print it out. You can do that at no cost from www.AnnualCreditReport.com. There, you can link to each of the three major credit bureaus—TransUnion, Experian, and Equifax—to get your annual free copy from each. Pick one, and follow the link to that site, where you'll have to answer some questions about your financial life to confirm your identity. Each bureau may have slightly different information, but for the purposes of this discussion, just one report from any of the bureaus will do fine. You can print out your report instantly. (And no, you can't get anyone else's report, because of the security questions involved.)

Now, pour a glass of wine, or maybe a cup of black coffee, and exchange credit reports. The report does not show your assets, only your use of credit over the past ten years. The bureaus simply gather the

Now, pour a glass of wine, or maybe a cup of black coffee, and exchange credit reports.

information reported to them by your card issuers, mortgage lender, and other companies, such as hospitals and doctors with whom you have accounts.

Years ago, credit reports were created in code, making them difficult to understand. But now you can see at a glance your partner's history of prompt payment, highest outstanding balance, and current balance on each account—as well as any past judgments, bankruptcies, or write-offs from lenders.

In this day and age, there is absolutely no reason to be hesitant to share your credit report with the person with whom you are planning to share your life. Being unwilling to share this information is more of a red flag than having negative information on the report. Remember, you can't pull your partner's credit report; only an individual (or a legitimate credit grantor) can gain access to this data. But a refusal to share this credit history would be a good reason to rethink tying your future life—personal, as well as financial—to this person.

That is not to say that a past bad credit history makes any person unsuitable for marriage or a long-term relationship. There may have been medical expenses, a previous divorce that involved an overspending spouse, or just financial ignorance involved in the past. What matters now is that your intended life partner has learned from experience and is ready and willing to enter this relationship with a clear conscience—and clear credit. Remember, your partner's credit history will easily become part of your own report as you start your life together, signing mortgage or rental agreements, registering utilities in both your names, or preparing a joint tax return.

STEP 5: REVIEW YOUR ASSETS – FULL DISCLOSURE

Now you're finally ready to approach the point in the discussion that most people think is the starting point for a prenuptial or cohabitation agreement on finances. You're ready to disclose your assets.

Courts have opined that to be fair—and to be upheld in a court of law—participants in a prenuptial agreement must fully disclose all their assets. That way, neither of the parties can claim to have signed the agreement without full knowledge of the situation. Not all states have laws specifically related to cohabitation agreements. Instead, these deals may be governed by general business law, which includes fraud provisions for contracts not made with full disclosure. Let's focus on the rules for a traditional prenup, while also considering these issues if you are cohabiting.

Sit down and make a list of all your assets. The list compiled by each of you will be attached to your prenuptial agreement. Include any equity in your home or in a business, as well as investments—even your retirement accounts. If you own stocks or valuable artwork or jewelry, now is the time to disclose them on the list. Will your intended be surprised? If he or she has already agreed to marry you, it shouldn't be an issue.

Remember, the idea of a prenuptial is partly to protect those assets that each of you brings into the marriage, in case it doesn't work.

There is always a way to structure an agreement based on full disclosure to keep those assets owned prior to the marriage, plus the income or appreciation derived from them during the marriage, as separate property. That's something you'll have to discuss with your prospective spouse and your attorney. But if you agree to keep some property separate, your agreement will have to specifically state that fact.

You may want to create a revocable living trust (RLT) and then retitle your premarital assets in the name of that trust. Then your agreement can simply specify that property held in your trust is not, and will not become, marital property. Even if you live in a community property state, where all property automatically becomes part of the marital estate, this type of agreement allows you to opt out of community property.

Retirement accounts may remain the property of the spouse who earned those benefits and out of reach of most creditors. Depending on state law, however, a spouse may be required to waive any statutory benefits to be a beneficiary of a retirement plan. In case of divorce, some states provide qualified domestic relations orders (QDROs) intended to equalize the marital assets and provide retirement benefits to a nonworking spouse in the case of a divorce. A properly drawn prenuptial agreement can identify retirement accounts—such as an IRA, 40l(k), or pension—as separate property. The agreement should specify that any future contributions to that account are also part of the separate property.

Similarly, most state laws provide that an *inheritance* remains the sole property of the beneficiary—even if the inheritance occurs during the marriage. However, that presumes you keep the inheritance separate. And that's a very important issue. If you ever make the mistake of commingling any separate property, you may no longer claim it as your own. If, for example, you inherit $50,000 and decide to pay down your joint mortgage, then that sum has become marital property.

So far, this discussion has revolved around your premarital assets and the concept of keeping them separate. But that's certainly not a requirement for any marriage or committed relationship. You might simply decide to *commingle* all your assets. It's a decision that only the two of you can make. But you should make it with the full knowledge that when you commingle assets, you may also be signing up for the acceptance of your partner's liabilities, including a damaged credit history.

STEP 6: DISCUSS ESTATE PLANNING

While we're talking about keeping property separate, it's time to bring up another unpleasant consideration: estate planning. You don't have to be wealthy to have an "estate." Even a young couple just starting out should consider the

You don't have to be wealthy to have an "estate."

possibilities. After all, even if your assets are titled jointly and you are each other's beneficiary for a retirement plan or life insurance, there could be some unpleasant consequences.

Suppose you are both fatally injured in an auto accident, but you die before your spouse. It's very possible that your mother-in-law could wind up with all your assets, since, absent a will—and children as heirs—she is your spouse's heir! And if you do have children, do you want your in-laws fighting over who will raise them, and how your assets will be spent to care for them? These are all issues that will be covered when you make your estate plan.

Couples with substantial assets, those who have children from a prior marriage, or those who have business partners will want to work with their estate-planning attorneys to protect the marital assets of each in case of death. Otherwise, state laws about who is entitled to a share of your assets will determine where your money goes after your death, except for life insurance and retirement accounts, which have named beneficiaries.

Estate-planning needs are dictated by both federal and state laws. State of residence is an important issue, because state law governs in many issues. As of this writing, the Supreme Court decision regarding same-sex marriages applies to the federal estate tax code—extending the tax-free transfer of assets to recognized same-sex spouses. However, the courts will determine which state laws apply to inheritances for state tax purposes. This is a quickly changing area of the law, and it is highly recommended that you choose an attorney who is a member of the bar in your state of residence to create your will and revocable living trust documents.

Later in this book, we'll give you some ideas on how to structure and protect assets that you agree to keep separate, while at the same time providing liquidity and financial security to your new spouse. But you can't do any effective planning if you are unwilling to share your true financial picture with your prospective partner. And what does it say about your relationship if you are unwilling to fully disclose your finances? Think about it.

What does it say about your relationship if you are unwilling to fully disclose your finances?

You've planned the wedding, created the guest list, and decided on the menu and the cake, or you've purchased a house together or signed a lease and shopped for furniture, because you're going to live together. If you would now take just a fraction of the time you spent on all those plans and start thinking about a money management plan, you'll be off to a much better start on your New Love Deal.

MONEY MANAGEMENT PLANNING

Have you thought about how you will manage your finances after you are together, and perhaps legally responsible for almost all of each other's debts, taxes, and other obligations? Here's a checklist that will help you get started on a money management plan. Some aspects of this plan may be formally included in your agreement; others may serve as an informal money management structure. In any case, they're worth a serious discussion.

- *Will you file a joint tax return?* You might need tax advice to make an informed decision. Married filing separately is a higher tax bracket, but there may be past IRS disputes, ongoing business arrangements, or other factors that would cause you to file separately. If you're just living together, this is a moot point. You will pay the tax rates that apply to singles—no matter what the Love Deal implies.

- *Will you deposit all your earnings into a joint checking account?* That may sound sensible and trusting, but certainly precludes any degree of financial privacy. Your partner will know exactly what you spent on that birthday or anniversary gift. An alternative would be to set up a household checking account to pay the regular bills. Retain the rest in separate accounts for your personal use.

- *Will you share household expenses equally or in proportion to your earnings?* Perhaps you'll decide that the one who earns more should contribute more to the joint household checking account. That doesn't mean the person who earns less—or retires or stays home to care for the children—isn't equally valuable in the financial equation.

- *Will you share joint use of a credit card?* That might be a good way to pay for joint expenses, when an appliance needs repair or the car breaks down. But can you trust that your partner isn't going to use his or her separate cards to ring up piles of debt?

- *Will you each contribute to your separate retirement accounts at work?* That answer is easy: each should have a separate retirement savings plan. Remember, even nonworking spouses can have an individual retirement account, easily set up through a bank or mutual fund company. That way, each can invest appropriately, depending on individual risk tolerances.

- *Whose health insurance policy will you use?* This is a tricky question. One plan may have obviously superior benefits, but how secure is that person's job? You'll need to do some serious comparisons to make this decision. It may pay to hang on to both policies, though you won't be able to collect from both. And different plans have different rules for covering unmarried partners or civil union spouses. Plus, as new health insurance rules take effect, there is less concern about being able to secure coverage in case of a job loss.

- *What's the plan for making major financial decisions?* Will you set a dollar amount for making major independent purchase decisions? How will you decide on priorities?

- *What's the plan for money given to former spouses, children, or aging parents?* This is one of the most contentious decisions in second marriages. If an ex-spouse is in dire need, is it fair to the current spouse to offer to help, especially if the extra money is being paid out of joint assets? When a grown child runs into financial problems, can parents give financial assistance out of their "own" money from before the marriage? Does the other spouse have any say in that decision? How will spending that money impact on joint plans—for a vacation home or long-planned trip? If you can't consider these questions now, they're sure to cause problems later.

- *Will either party be obligated to pay off the other's debts?* Whether it is student loans or credit card bills from before marriage, it is important to sort this out. If one spouse pays for living expenses, while the other uses his or her income to pay down debt, there is a potential for conflict that is better discussed and resolved in advance.

These are just some of the financial questions and issues that are likely to arise in any marriage. If your current state of engaged bliss can't tolerate this type of discussion, then your relationship may be too fragile to survive in the long run. It's better to know now than later. But most likely, if you follow the steps in this chapter, you will have set up a solid framework to openly discuss and manage money issues, respecting each other's values and privacy in the process.

Chapter 8:

PRENUP DEAL POINTS

We freely admit that it is more fun to talk about feelings, emotions, and celebrity stories than it is to talk about law. But a prenuptial agreement is a legal and enforceable contract. It is an agreement with long-term consequences for both love and money, so we have to be serious about understanding how it works.

First comes love, then comes a prenuptial agreement, but in between those two, you have to educate yourself as to what your legal rights and responsibilities to each other would be without a prenuptial agreement. Don't feel overwhelmed. All you need to understand is enough about the law to ask the right questions, so you can control the lawyers involved and protect your love.

In chapter 10 we will give you some advice on choosing an appropriate lawyer. But you need to know some basic rules when it comes to creating a valid prenuptial agreement. They can be summarized as follows:

RULE #1: *Marital law is state law for the most part, and you need to know if your state falls into one of three categories:*

a) Is it a *community property* state? This assumes that all property acquired by the spouses during marriage belongs not to either spouse individually but to a fictional third entity called the "marital community." In that entity, each party has an equal and identical interest. Generally, in community property states, property is divided equally if the marriage is dissolved. In a divorce, some community property states—such as Arizona, Idaho, Nevada, Texas, and Washington—are moving toward an "equitable" (i.e., fair and just under the circumstances) rather than an exact equal property division. In other community property states—namely California, Louisiana, and New Mexico—property on divorce is still divided equally.

b) Is it an *equitable distribution* (rather than community property) state? This allows a divorce court to apportion the marital estate not necessarily equally, but rather in an equitable and just manner. Equity, like beauty, is in the eyes of the beholder, but generally, it means "fairly" considering various factors, such as health, responsibilities, and earning power of each party. Most states use some application of the equitable distribution approach.

c) Is your state governed by the *Uniform Marital Property Act* (UMPA)? Currently, Wisconsin is the only state that uses this hybrid system of property classification, which is a sort of cross between equitable distribution and community property.

Speaking generally, every state has a concept of marital property: property acquired *during* the marriage belongs to the marriage.

Nonmarital property is generally property acquired by gift or inheritance, either before or during the marriage—or whatever property you two decide to *exclude* from marital property through your prenuptial agreement. Additionally, your state law might define other property to be nonmarital.

In most equitable distribution states, your nonmarital property is relatively safe as your "own," but it is safer still when listed as part of a prenuptial agreement. Importantly, if you change your legal residence during your marriage and subsequently divorce in another state, absent a written agreement, you might find that your nonmarital property has been inadvertently converted in status.

Again, speaking broadly, in every state, there is a right for spouses to be supported by each other during a marriage and maybe even after divorce, depending on the length of the marriage and other factors. Of course, minor children have a right to be supported by both biological parents during, after, and even before a marriage.

The legal concepts are not that complicated, although the differences between states and how they apply those concepts can be daunting. It is amazing how little attention most of us pay to these rights and rules when launching into and living in a married life.

Bottom line: the best guarantee of a legally enforceable contract is to work with knowledgeable lawyers who are admitted to the bar in your state of residence. Even if you subsequently move with your spouse to another state, *as long as your prenup agreement clearly states that*

The best guarantee of a legally enforceable contract is to work with knowledgeable lawyers

the rules of your original state of residence will apply, you will be protected by it.

RULE# 2: *Not only does state law vary as to what your rights are as a married couple, but state laws also vary as to how they view prenuptial agreements.*

States vary as to their recognition and application of premarital agreements. Twenty-five states and the District of Columbia have adopted the Uniform Premarital Agreement Act. Under the UPAA, it is now easier to enforce a premarital agreement than it used to be. In summary, this Act (not to be confused with the Uniform Marital Property Act) provides a definition of the agreement between two people who are marrying and their property rights, and requires that the agreement be in writing and signed. It lists the various assets and income about which you are able to make agreements, and really only prohibits parties from agreements that violate the law or public policy or that would adversely impact a child's right to support. Its toughest provisions favor enforcement and narrowly define the circumstances under which a premarital agreement would not be enforced.

The states that have formally adopted the UPAA are: Arizona, Arkansas, California, Connecticut, Delaware, the District of Columbia, Hawaii, Idaho, Illinois, Indiana, Iowa, Kansas, Maine, Montana, Nebraska, Nevada, New Jersey, New Mexico, North Carolina, North Dakota, Oregon, Rhode Island, South Dakota, Texas, Utah, and Virginia. And even those states that have not formally adopted the act seem to be moving toward applying its principles and preferences for enforcement.

RULE #3: *You can put almost anything you want into your prenup, but the courts may only enforce certain provisions.*

The most obvious topic that comes to mind is the care and custody of children. Certainly, it is important to discuss how you plan to deal with custody of any children you have together, as well as the amount of child support either of you will or will not pay. Remember, though, that issues relating to children are always and forever within the court's jurisdiction, so long as the children are minors (or in post-

Issues relating to children are always and forever within the court's jurisdiction,

high-school education). If the two of you do not agree, your input on these topics will be, at best, a statement of your thoughts and interests at the time you drafted the agreement. Child support issues are not the "law" of your divorce.

Another area in which the court may intervene relates to monthly support or maintenance. In cases where one spouse would be left destitute or in penury and dependent on the government, a judge might order some kind of mandated support, despite the provisions of your prenuptial agreement.

If you discussed the financial issues presented in the previous chapter, you have a good idea about some of the deal points regarding financial assets that you might want in your prenup agreement. Make a list, and don't avoid this discussion. Whether it's about assets you have before marriage, assets built up during the marriage, or the division of assets after the potential end of your marriage, it's better to plan in advance. In chapter 12, Terry has some suggestions for dealing with financial issues that might arise depending on your situation.

Rather than being exposed to the decisions of an unpredictable court system, we would advise trusting yourself and each other.

Work together to make a fair arrangement, and one that has flexibility or can be modified if there are substantial changes in circumstances for either of you—be it your health, your income, or your children.

Pay very close attention to the cautionary words of one Illinois judge who, in 1972, expressed what many judges believe: "Courts cannot make for the parties better agreements than they themselves have been satisfied to make." In short, the deal you make is the deal you take. Don't count on a judge weighing in to improve your lot.

As you can see, a prenup can cover some broad territory. And while couples may also incorporate other, more personal provisions (for example, weight gain or infidelity), it will be difficult to get a court to enforce some of those portions of the agreement relating to them.

DO IT RIGHT

Those three basic rules devolve into much legalese—but the basics are pretty simple. Since a prenuptial agreement is the right thing to do, and since there are apparently no easy escape clauses (see next chapter), let's do it right.

Your agreement needs to be voluntarily done in written form. There are standard disclosures that are part of every contract. They include: who you are, where you live, your ages and employment, the date of your upcoming wedding, your purpose in writing in this agreement, your marital history (if any), and the status and residence of your already-born children (if any).

Other key ingredients to your contract include: how long this premarital agreement will last; under what circumstances it may terminate, in whole or in part; how you will amend it in the future; and which state's law you choose to have applied to this agreement and its future interpretation, no matter what your state of residence at the time you may split up.

The agreement will also contain a listing of each of your full disclosures. Generally speaking, those include all your assets and your liabilities.

FULL DISCLOSURE

If you remember anything at all from this section, please remember two words: *full disclosure*. Those words, *full disclosure*, should be the mantra for both of you, for three significant reasons:

1. It is critical to the legality of your prenuptial agreement.

2. It is critical to the foundation of your relationship.

3. It is essential, because if you ever proceed to court to litigate this deal, the judge will assume that each of you could have, and should have, known about all assets when the agreement was made.

SEPARATE LEGAL REPRESENTATION

In chapter 10 we have some extensive advice about choosing an attorney to represent you in crafting this document. Suffice it to say, while you want an advocate, you do not want one who creates such disharmony that your love is destroyed in the process.

So you want to get along. But don't make the mistake of choosing an attorney in the same law firm as the one representing your betrothed, just for the sake of convenience. You need separate, competent, and unconflicted advice in this process.

Those are the basics of drafting a prenuptial agreement. We didn't intend to make you a lawyer! That's why you need competent representation. You need the facts, not myths, going into this process. The next chapter is designed to bust those myths about prenups—and give you a dose of reality.

KEY DEAL POINTS

- Full disclosure is absolutely essential.

- Separate legal representation is required.

- Marital law is state law.

- Different states regard prenups differently.

- Court decisions supersede prenup provisions with regard to minor children.

- Don't believe prenup "myths."

Chapter 9:

BEWARE OF MYTHICAL THINKING

Because the law of property and marital rights, as well as the approach to prenuptial agreements, has evolved over time, major myths have developed. Myths about legal rights are dangerous because they lull us into a false sense of security. We find out too late that we knew too little!

Some of those misconceptions about prenuptial agreements revolve around the ability to contract for specific provisions that may be contrary to law or public policy. Others are "urban legends" about coercion and legal representation. It's important to sort out these myths from the facts as they have been developed through litigation in every state.

Many people think they know the law from watching movies and television. But don't believe everything you see or hear—especially about prenups. What hurts you most might be what you think you

But don't believe everything you see or hear—especially about prenups.

know that isn't so! Here are some of the most prevalent prenuptial myths:

MYTH #L: *Prenuptial agreements are easily broken.*

Fact: As a matter of fact, almost the polar opposite is true. All the political, social, economic, and legal pressures favor the principle that "the deal you make is the deal you take." The Uniform Prenuptial Agreement Act closes many, if not most, of the legal loopholes through which an unhappy spouse used to escape.

MYTH #2: *If I avoid having a lawyer of my own, no one can hold me to my agreement.*

Fact: Since I am an attorney, it may look like I am being self-serving when I advise you to consult an attorney of your own, especially if you are the younger or less wealthy partner. I am not trying to create more legal work. The fact is that of you can choose to proceed without an attorney, but if you do, you will be stuck with the consequences of what you may not have known, understood, or intended.

The concept here is that if you could have had an attorney (and everybody could) and chose not to have one, you knowingly gave up legal advice and are bound by your own agreement. Perhaps you did not have an attorney so you would not upset your beloved, because you felt there was not enough time or you feared negotiating, or for lots of other real-life reasons. Even so, with only few exceptions (such as care of a child), your deal is your deal.

MYTH #3: *My partner is just doing this because his or her parents/ children/boss insist, but he or she will take care of me later.*

Fact: Once you have executed a premarital agreement that feels confiscatory or minimalist for one side or the other, the odds of it being rewritten after the marriage are not good. Your odds of winning the lottery or realizing a wish upon a star are better. The best moments for open, transparent, and fair dealing are before you sign on the dotted line, not after.

MYTH #4: *If I do not take any interest in the asset disclosures and values and just go along to get along, I can always plead ignorance later.*

Fact: Trying to play dumb is truly ignorant and will backfire. Sure, you can ignore the facts and not be conversant with the balance sheet, but the courts will not only ask if you knew, but also if you could have known and chose not to. If either of these is true—you knew or could have known—you may be locked into the deal.

Litigation over prenuptial agreements is treacherous, and the person trying to invalidate one will not be rewarded for using ignorance as a shield and a sword. Rarely will the judges buy this argument unless there is actual and substantial fraud.

MYTH #5: *If we have already announced the wedding date, made deposits on the wedding and honeymoon sites, invited the guests, accepted their gifts, and, God forbid, are actually at the engagement party or already in the church vestibule, my signature is meaningless, as I was clearly under duress.*

Fact: Don't be too sure. Courtrooms can be cold and judgmental places. Obviously, the further along you are with your public commitment, the more likely that a court will at least hear your cries of duress. However, the decision to marry is a uniquely personal one. On that basis, there are courts in these very situations that have judged you just could have said no to the prenuptial and no to the wedding, and those courts have chosen to uphold what appear to be unfair agreements.

In the real world, we all know calling off a wedding that is days or even weeks away is emotionally and financially unthinkable, if not almost impossible. In the legal world, it is not only possible but advisable. If you think that either you or your intended may want or need a prenuptial, the idea is to start early so that you do not have any danger of a shotgun prenuptial that might be unfair but legally enforced.

SOME TITILLATING PROVISIONS THAT MAY OR MAY NOT ACTUALLY BE ENFORCEABLE

While we're on the subject of myths, let's destroy one overwhelming myth—the belief that a prenup can govern an unlimited range of desires. You might agree, for example, to maintain a certain weight range, but no court could enforce this provision!

All the really good stories about love and money come from the entertainment field. The stakes are big, and the emotions are bigger. Can these contracts be enforced? It will be up to the courts to decide—if the couple decides to divorce!

Celebrities frequently have premarital clauses setting large fines and/or bonuses for really bad behavior, such as adultery. Apparently, if you can prove it, you can collect it, and rarely are you pressed to prove it! A truly controlling "star-nup" reportedly required that neither party would make disparaging remarks about the personal, private, or family life of the other, including the other's family, companions, dates, acquaintances, or future spouses. What is left to talk about?

There are some prenup demands that probably are not enforceable, but are interesting examples of ways we have seen people be controlling, egocentric, and even desperate. Here are just a few of those provisions, and, truly, we could not have made them up!

Wife limited her husband to watching one football game with friends.

Mothers-in-law were barred from sleepover visits.

Husband had to curb his tongue around the in-laws, or he would be fined $10,000 every time he was rude.

The couple could spend no longer than two consecutive days with the in-laws.

Wife paid a $500 fine for every pound gained.

Husband's maximum weight restricted to 180 pounds.

Spouse must submit to random drug testing with fines for positive results.

One deal specified how long the husband could work before he retired.

Agreement on which religion the children would follow, which school the children would attend.

The couple agreed not to have children.

Agreement stated how often the couple would have sex.

One declared all frequent flier miles go to the spouse who remained faithful.

Spouses specified who got custody of the pets, and even the housekeeper!

Now, don't go getting any crazy ideas on your own. Your lawyer will tell you what is legally enforceable, as opposed to simply a personal agreement about behaviors. But do remember that whatever you agree to put into your document might someday be raised publicly in a court of law, even if a judge does not enforce that provision.

Now you know the difference between the myths and reality, between legally enforceable provisions and the deal points you and your spouse might choose privately, although they are unlikely to be enforced in court. Yes, your agreement can include both aspects of your arrangement, but the resolution of the courts is not likely to be binding on some of your most outrageous demands upon each other! So don't get caught up in the social deal points, to the extent that you forget the importance of the financial arrangements that could be most costly in a future dispute.

Once you understand that balance, you're ready to consult attorneys. But not just "any" attorney. Read the next chapter for some important advice.

DISCUSS *YOUR* DEMANDS

Now that you know the difference between myths and reality, take a moment to think of some of the deal points that are probably too frivolous to be put into your agreement. But if you could make such requests or demands of your beloved, what would they be? Make a list of what you would like to request.

Once you've made your list, review it carefully. Are your demands so significant and intrusive that you might want to rethink their future impact on your relationship? After all, you know how hard it is to change yourself.

Your Love Deal can specify facts and numbers, and create a framework to deal with specifics. But it can't change your inherent personality traits, or those of your partner.

Chapter 10:

LAWYERS, LOVE, AND MEDIATION

"I called three times and you never called me back, never returned my phone calls. I sent you the documents over two weeks ago, and no response."

"Why would I respond to documents that are a complete insult? I am offended by that proposal."

Surprise! These are not the parties arguing, but an exchange between the lawyers who are supposed to help couples negotiate a sustaining marriage contract in a collaborative and relationship-enhancing way. Before selecting a wedding location, choosing a menu, and creating an invitation list, couples should choose a lawyer to help them prepare a prenup.

Choosing a lawyer for most people is a process that creates anxiety and uses up emotional reserves. Many people believe that lawyers thrive on conflict. They find it difficult to imagine that attorneys could possess the skills that would be required in this type of delicate negotiation. They wonder if there is a lawyer who could maintain the gentleness that love bestows upon the parties, while at the same time protecting them against the very person who is soon to swear "to love, honor, and protect" them.

If you're concerned about these potential distortions of your relationship as you prepare to create an agreement that will provide the framework for your life together, there is another approach. To be sure, you will eventually need separate attorneys to ratify your decisions. But, as you'll see later in this chapter, the services of a mediator can be very useful in coming to agreement on your deal issues—before the lawyers start negotiation your contract. In fact, your attorney may help you find a professional mediator.

Prenuptial contracts have a disturbing effect for a reason. A loved one, who has become vital to one's sense of happiness and well-being, may be offended by the requests made. One fears degeneration of those good feelings and, ultimately, of one's own happiness if the process becomes hostile.

Hopefully, you've used the checklists in the earlier chapters to each come up with, and start a discussion of, your deal points. That will give your lawyers a place to start, and areas of agreement that can form the basis for your prenup. But this is the time to tell your own lawyer of your fears and concerns, as well as any disagreements that have already surfaced. Lawyers have seen it all before—and they know how to make deals work.

There is a justifiable fear of suffering from failed expectations about the reactions of a partner to requests, and then, what to do if requests are denied. The inherent conflict is the desire to protect

The inherent conflict is the desire to protect your financial future at the same time as striving to protect your happiness.

your financial future at the same time as striving to protect your happiness.

It is our belief that these are not mutually exclusive, and with wisely chosen allies, the turbulent waters can be navigated.

FINDING THE "RIGHT" ATTORNEY

A divorce attorney friend of mine admitted, "I never understood why people were so emotional about their prenuptial agreements until I was negotiating my own and found myself sobbing for hours in the bathtub." Subsequently, she has completely changed her approach to handling these cases.

Finding a good attorney can be fraught with challenges. Couples should begin by using the same types of resources they would use to find any professional. Family and friends are typically excellent resources. Couples can also contact their local bar association to obtain a list of attorneys who specialize in family law. A trusted family attorney or estate planner who may not have had enough experience in prenuptial or relationship contracts to do one may be all too happy to make a referral. Some estate-planning attorneys, however, do have experience in this field.

Each person should interview several attorneys to determine which one is the right fit for each of them. It's time-consuming but essential in finding not only a qualified attorney, but one who reflects the couple's sensibilities.

Because it's challenging to know what to ask attorneys to flush out their true sentiments, we will raise some helpful issues to ask about as you talk with a potential attorney. The answers to these questions should reveal the quality of the attorney's past experience and how he or she will behave in this emotionally fragile and potentially explosive negotiation.

Of course, you're starting with an attorney who has been recommended as an expert in crafting prenuptial agreements. But it doesn't hurt to ask about the depth of an attorney's experience, his or her attitude toward these documents, and how the attorney typically handles disagreements in the negotiation of the document. Also, ask if the lawyer has any objection to working with a mediator or a financial planner in the process.

You should be interested in the attorney's reputed temperament. A highly combative attorney is not the best type for these situations, unless the attorney can access another inner dimension. Even the most aggressive will tell you they have an accommodating side. On the other hand, many attorneys have malpractice concerns that cause them to be especially aggressive in this type of negotiation. It's worth asking whether this will impact their negotiations on your behalf.

If you don't feel comfortable with the lawyer from the beginning, it is doubtful that things will get better. Lawyers have their best foot forward at the initial meeting. Don't be afraid to trust your instincts.

Finally, make sure that the attorneys you choose will actually be handling the case and will not turn it over to a less experienced associate. And never consider sharing one attorney. As with any legal topic, the potential for a full-blown dispute requires that each have an attorney to represent her or him separately.

No matter how strong the connection is with a chosen attorney, you should discuss the question of fees and expenses. This is true regardless of who is paying the bill. Typically, an attorney charges an hourly rate for services, a lesser hourly rate for any associate attorneys that may be working on the agreement, and direct costs (faxes, copies, et cetera). Inquire about telephone consultations and how they are calculated. Remember, if you use the attorney to do a lot of emotional hand-holding, it will increase your bill. This is where expenses can add up, but remember, what attorneys are "selling" is their time and experience.

No matter how strong the connection is with a chosen attorney, you should discuss the question of fees and expenses

It can be difficult for an attorney to estimate the amount of time to be spent on a project. For a prenup, the cost generally starts around $2,500 and could go much higher, depending on the size of the estate or the size of the conflict that must be negotiated.

Before making the final decision about a lawyer, couples should take time for contemplation. They should ask themselves the ultimate question: "Given my personality, do I need a stronger lawyer who will play tough and take the heat for me, or do I have a need to be in control of the lawyer?"

THE ADVANTAGE OF MEDIATORS

Mediation can be an excellent resource for helping couples and their lawyers negotiate this unique agreement. A lawyer may be trained in advocacy, but a mediator is trained in peacemaking. The goal of advocacy is to protect one party; the goal of mediation is the comfort offered by its neutrality and equalization of bargaining power. Many, if not all, of the issues in a prenuptial agreement have an emotional component.

Mediation can be an excellent resource for helping couples and their lawyers negotiate this unique agreement.

Let's not automatically assume that the creation of a prenuptial agreement for a loving couple must necessarily involve dispute resolution. Our goal in this book is to bring you together to discuss and deal with the issues your relationship will confront. But the process is bound to bring differences into perspective. Most can be resolved by compromise, a simple back-and-forth between two willing attorneys who consult their clients and are resolved to get the deal done with as little conflict as possible. But if you suspect that something you—or your partner—is proposing is a deal-breaker, then you might want to enlist the services of a trained mediator right from the start.

Mediators are trained to handle this engagement, rather than shy away from it. Different professionals with different backgrounds may be retained. What is important is that they are trained and qualified to mediate. The predominant goal in prenups is financial protection and settlements. For this reason, the mediator should be an attorney assisted, if necessary, by a financial planner and/or a therapist.

In the process of mediating an agreement, with either a mediator or therapist, couples are likely to learn or develop better communication skills that they may continue to use throughout their marriage.

A therapist can also help with the problematic aspects of blending new stepfamilies together. Both partners can have their lawyers present at these sessions, but the primary voices will be their own.

Mediators can be recommended by your respective attorneys, or by searching the directory at www.Mediate.com. If you do decide to use a mediator, you still need to each be represented by an attorney, to review, analyze, and write up the agreement you made with the help of a mediator. As we have previously emphasized, you need two attorneys for the agreement to be safely held up in court.

Michele explains why after nearly twenty years on the bench, she has become a sought-after mediator in marital relations issues. She has not escaped the divorce wars with this career turn. Rather, she is intent on defusing them. Her thoughts on the subject:

Mediation is one of the most important tools that exist to resolve conflict from the mundane to the monumental. So deeply do I hold this belief that I have made a career change, taking training at Harvard University, and have just retired from the bench to become a full-time mediator. For people negotiating financial contracts where love is the overriding factor I can't imagine a better strategy. The commonly used adversarial model for negotiating prenuptial agreements deters many from considering them, and limits the benefits that couples might otherwise achieve by prenuptial planning.

Another reason that I find mediation so compelling is that the conflict that might be unleashed in the creation of a prenup often has less to do with the issues, and more to do with miscommunication. Let's face it, people are afraid that they won't handle or finesse the situation well. People tell me they are also afraid of their own temper and capacity for doing damage. The fear can go from being a speed bump to a road block to asking for a prenup. The goal of mediation is to resolve disputes amicably and protect communication in the process. The goal is neutrality rather than advocacy. The goal is for both parties to be—and feel—protected.

Trained mediators are sensitive to power imbalances and know how to neutralize power plays. They are trained to uncover and clarify each party's hidden interests. Their role is to foster trust in a controlled, safe setting. They are experts at setting timelines and meeting deadlines, without rushing the process. In other words, mediators act to maintain a positive emotional terrain by controlling or defusing negative emotions or attacks, enforcing behavioral ground rules, and keeping parties focused on the issues that the mediator helps identify.

Trained mediators are sensitive to power imbalances and know how to neutralize power plays.

For all these reasons, mediation can set the course not only for a good prenuptial agreement, but for a good long-term relationship. And that is my goal in every situation I am called upon to mediate.

When couples have completed mediation, they will have a document often referred to as a memorandum of understanding. This is the document that their respective attorneys will utilize to create the legal contract between them. Mediators often work with the attorneys to negotiate the agreement, bringing nuance to the process and making sure that what has been agreed upon in mediation is reflected in the document. Still, at the end of the process you must read your contract carefully, ask questions if you are confused about any of the clauses or wording, and feel comfortable that you are getting the deal you can live with over the years.

FINANCIAL PLANNERS CAN HELP

In the next two chapters, you'll find some examples about how to structure the financial aspects of your deal, using life insurance, trusts, taxes, and gifts. While these are extensive examples designed to make you aware of some of these techniques, a Certified Financial Planner (CFP) may help you create other strategies applicable to your situation. You can search for these planners at www.CFPBoard.org.

Since you are not yet officially a legal couple, each might want to have separate financial advisors—especially if the amount of money is large and the issues are complex. A good place to start the search for advice is to find a *fee-only planner,* one who is not trying to sell you any products (although he or she may recommend certain products to fund your deal). Go to www.FeeOnly.org to search for a Certified Financial Planner who will work on a fee basis to review or help create your Love Deal.

Your planner is likely to come up with creative ways to either equalize or protect assets, lending financial certainty and peace of mind to your agreement.

COLLABORATIVE LAW

Collaborative law is a new and growing specialty that is designed to mellow the adversarial process of negotiating all kinds of deals. It may work especially well in dealing with domestic relations, when the parties are willing to work toward a common goal, such as creating a prenup, or even dissolving a union with a minimum of bitterness and cost.

The aim of collaborative law is to have lawyers represent their individual clients, but collaborate on solutions that will best resolve problems. It might seem that, at least for certain disputes, the idea of both sides working together to reach a fair conclusion could be an improvement over a long court battle. Certainly, the process of reaching an appropriate prenuptial deal should benefit from appropriate collaboration between attorneys representing separate parties.

CONTROLLING YOUR LAWYER – AND YOURSELF!

With or without a lawyer, there are certain similarities in negotiating with a partner. Knowing what they are in advance helps you to avoid the inherent challenges of this process or even avert disaster. You, not your lawyer, will live with the result of your negotiations.

If a lawyer behaves in a way that is not representative of how you want to remember yourself in the long run, it's your job to tighten the reins. A lawyer's job is to be an adversary, to be intimidating when necessary, and to help a client feel empowered. As time goes on, you will find it more difficult to hide behind your attorney's behavior and may, in time, feel some remorse. Your relationship comes first. If attorneys are creating a hostile situation, you may need to call a détente. It is your job to communicate to the lawyer what behavior is not acceptable.

There are times during prenuptial negotiations when one of you may feel as if you no longer know your mate. Whenever possible, you must try to keep the lines of communication with your partner open, because then, at least, you are negotiating one-on-one instead of five-on-one.

One of you may be anxious to get the signing of the document over and done with, putting pressure on the other to sign quickly. But the requests and legalities contained in the document take time to digest. If one of you signs before you are ready, you may be dissatisfied later because you signed under pressure. You and your partner should respect each other's need for reflection on this agreement. Ideally, you should start the process months before you marry or move in.

If one of you signs before you are ready, you may be dissatisfied later because you signed under pressure.

One final thought: each of you should take a snapshot of your behavior during negotiations. Is this how you want to remember yourself? Is this how you want to be remembered by your partner?

FINDING PROFESSIONAL HELP

- Get separate attorneys, skilled at prenups, by searching state bar association sites or asking professionals, or experienced friends for recommendations

- Interview attorneys carefully

- Ask about fees, and decide who will pay

- Come prepared with a list of deal points

- Consider using a mediator, therapist, financial planner

- CONTROL your attorney!

Chapter 11:

THE ART OF THE DEAL – FINDING FAIRNESS

It's time to work out the financial details of your agreement. Every situation is different, individual, and personal. So your challenge is to understand your goals, both near-term and long-term, and then be creative in reaching them with the least cost, conflict, and confusion possible.

In this chapter, you'll find a variety of strategies that you can employ together to create the financial portion of your agreement. In addition to consulting with your attorneys, you might want to contact a Certified Financial Planner as suggested in chapter 10. (You can find one in your area by doing an online search at www.CFPBoard. org.) They are experts at understanding the long-term consequences of decisions and deals that you make today.

But, as we advise throughout this book, don't get buried in the details and lose sight of your main objective: *financial fairness.*

Don't get buried in the details and lose sight of your main objective: financial fairness.

Fairness is in the eye of the beholder, but one thing is sure: financial fairness is not the same as financial equality. The idea behind "fairness" is to come to an agreement about an equitable way to deal with three financial categories: previous assets; current income and assets accumulated *during* the marriage or relationship; and then an equitable distribution of assets if the marriage or relationship does not work out, or in case of death. To put it simply, you need to make a plan that deals with past, present, and future.

For sure, you don't want to leave the issue of fairness up to the courts, which is what will happen absent a written agreement, made with the advice of separate lawyers for each party. Any deal you make at the start is likely to be more equitable than a judge might be compelled to make at the finish.

In its simplest terms, the question of fairness is as follows: If a hypothetical Tess is married to a hypothetical Tom and they amass $100 million of marital money over a long and hardworking marriage, does it belong to each of them fifty-fifty, or should whoever actually earned the money (be it Tess or Tom) be allowed to keep the greater portion, while the other gets "more than enough" money for the rest of his or her life?

As with everything in law, the answer can vary depending on where you live, which judge is hearing your case, and, to some extent, the contribution each partner made to the success of the other. Partly, the answer varies because we as a society are not sure what we believe to be "fair." The ultimate answer is as unique and varied as a fingerprint. And take it from Michele, the judge, who says the challenge is just to make sure the decision comes "within the fairness ballpark." In other words, unless you define fairness in your agreement, you cannot predict the specifics of a deal worked out in court.

Ironically, it was another General Electric executive divorce that first highlighted this question in 1997. Gary Wendt was the chief of GE Capital Corp. His wife, Lorna, had been married to him for thirty-two years and had apparently been the quintessential corporate wife—tirelessly traveling and entertaining. He offered her what he thought was "enough" for her, but she battled for half of everything—and won a $20 million divorce judgment. She then began The Institute for Equality in Marriage (www.equalityinmarriage.org), and the debate over what is "fair"—either "enough" or "equality"—has raged on to this very day.

The New Love Deal lesson is that an agreement between the two partners is more reliable than any litigation outcome. Otherwise, where you live and an unknown judge will interpret your life and determine your unpredictable future based on his or her idea of "fairness."

EQUALITY VERSUS FAIRNESS

Why not strive for equality? The answer to that question is that true financial equality is impossible. Couples, whether living together or planning for marriage, come to the relationship with their own financial assets—and liabilities. Wealth or age may be unequal. Earning power, past and future, may not be evenly balanced.

Children from previous marriages or those anticipated in the current marriage may not have equal financial needs. There may be preexisting commitments to support a lifestyle for a previous spouse. Inheritances may contribute to your lifestyle but may not be considered marital assets. Existing estate plans and life insurance beneficiaries may need to be revised to complement your new pre-nuptial agreement.

DIVIDING TIME, DIVIDING MONEY

Just think: *past, present, and future.* As you work on your agreement, those three time frames will become clear. If each of you came into the relationship with no past, no assets, no children, and no credit history, then you can avoid thinking about or revealing your financial past. But that's rarely the case.

Just think: past, present, and future

The present is the term of your togetherness—whether forever, until death parts you, or in case you divorce or legally separate. It is the time period where the "deal" is in force and your plans are enacted and fulfilled. In chapter 7, you gained the tools for organizing your ongoing financial life—whether paying household bills, saving for retirement, planning for vacations and shared goals, or simply deciding who pays for dinner at that expensive restaurant.

Now, use that shared knowledge to plan what will happen if you're not together at some time in the future when the relationship deal ends for one reason or another. How can you create a fair ending? Can you agree now that if either of you feels the marriage or relationship is not working out that you will seek joint counseling? Is it appropriate to agree that the moment one party notifies the other, in writing, of a desire to end the relationship, the prenup or cohab agreement will be automatically triggered?

Advance planning about these details will avoid arguments about when the relationship ended, when financial arrangements are put into effect to separate assets, and when the clock starts ticking to a division of assets or income. You will have prepared for a future that you hope never arrives.

If you plan for those contingencies—death, incapacity, or divorce—now, you can look forward to your financial future with better security, knowing that at least you won't have expensive legal bills at the end. Details, details! There are so many details and situations that it's tempting just to give up on the idea of planning in advance. That would be your most significant mistake. The little things that you let slip under the glow of romance are the ones most likely to cause trouble in the future. So let's get started.

The little things that you let slip under the glow of romance are the ones most likely to cause trouble in the future.

REVEALING ASSETS

As we noted previously, the basis for any agreement is full and complete disclosure of existing assets and liabilities. Without full disclosure, there may well be no agreement—or at least not an enforceable one.

So that's where you must start if you want your prenuptial or cohabitation agreement—and the trust basis for your relationship—to move forward. It's time for each of you to make another list. This doesn't have to be done by an accountant or tax professional, although that might be important in the case of great wealth.

The definition of *assets* is anything you own, either outright or in partnership. So if you own real estate, you'll list its current value, and also the amount of any mortgage or home equity loans taken out against the value of that real estate. If you own a car, you should disclose your loan amount.

List the value of your stocks, mutual funds, and expensive artwork that you might have collected. List the certificates of deposit or money in the bank. If you own life insurance that has a cash value, it should be disclosed. If you are the beneficiary of any trusts, or if your family trusts provide for your children's college educations, that, too, should be added to your list. It might be appropriate to get a professional appraisal for the current value of artwork and similar items, or you might value it based on the stated value in your property insurance policy.

If you have a retirement account, that will remain separate by law. However, in a contested divorce, the value of retirement assets might be used to create a balanced division of assets. In contemplating an agreement, you'll also want to disclose the value of your IRA or 401(k) plan at work, as part of the full-disclosure process.

Once you're married, your spouse has a legal right to benefits from your 401(k) or pension plan. So if you've agreed to keep those assets separate, the spouse must sign a waiver for the trustees of the retirement plan. Also, the contributions you make to a retirement plan after you are married are not protected as a separate asset, unless your agreement specifically states that fact. Certainly, some things are priceless. Treasured mementos from your family would fall into this category, but because they have special sentimental value, you might want to make note of them. If you collect baseball cards or antique jewelry, you should simply list the collection at an estimated value. That will remind you, as part of your agreement, to keep those items as separate property. But if they will require maintenance or insurance, you should pay for those expenses out of your separate property, not out of marital assets.

Keeping premarital assets separate is a legal task that may require the creation of trusts to segregate those assets. But remember, this is a discussion of *fairness*. Now that you've highlighted your own separate assets, this list could be the foundation of a discussion of fair treatment of either party in the future, in case the marriage fails. Whether the issue is support, maintenance, or gifting of assets, you can't get to fairness without an honest statement.

TIME – THE PRICELESS ASSET

The one asset upon which you cannot put a price is your time, your life—the hours that you spend together that can never be regained or redivided. Those may be hours spent building a business or moving away from a career. How to fairly compensate each other for those lost opportunities or the support given to create opportunities is a discussion that can never revolve around a simple mathematical balance sheet. And it may be the most difficult to appropriately value unless you do it at a time when you are most in agreement about each other's true worth.

The one asset upon which you cannot put a price is your time,

A special note: it is especially important to consider the fairness of dividing assets if you are not creating a legal marriage, where dissolution of the relationship will largely depend on state civil laws and lawyers to interpret them if you cannot agree. But a cohabitation agreement and even a civil union are likely to have far less precedent in court in case your deal falls apart. So, as you create your agreement, think carefully about the assets each of you brings to the relationship and how you would fairly divide your lives if things don't work out.

DISCLOSING LIABILITIES

Don't forget about your liabilities or debts. The obvious ones are credit card debts and mortgages. But you may also have cosigned a loan for a family member or you may have student loans. Detail each loan or debt separately, along with the interest rate and repayment terms. If you've ever filed for bankruptcy, that fact should definitely be disclosed at this point. If you haven't done so already, you'll likely be exchanging credit reports, so much of this information will be revealed anyway.

There is a different kind of debt that should also be disclosed on this list. It's called future obligations. Have you promised to pay for college for children from a previous marriage? Do you owe support to an ex-spouse until he or she reaches a certain age or remarries? Do you make payments on a life insurance policy that benefits your kids or ex? Do you expect that you and your siblings will have to chip in to pay for nursing care for an aging parent? These are all financial considerations that might have a bearing on your lifestyle and future planning, so they should be fully disclosed.

Don't be embarrassed about revealing your financial situation. Remember, if you've followed our

If you're having an intimate relationship, you'll have to be willing to expose your personal finances.

advice, you've already had some frank discussions about money just to get ready for your deal documents. If you're having an intimate relationship, you'll have to be willing to expose your personal finances.

Now that you've revealed your financial past and present, it's time to structure your deal for your future together. The truth is in the details, and it's easy to get overwhelmed since you're now considering not only ways to make your deal work—but the possibilities if it doesn't. While no one strategy will work in all cases, in the following chapter you will get some ideas of how you can plan for success. Whether doing the basic planning with your partner, or working with your attorney and your financial advisor in complicated cases, it pays to understand the techniques and alternatives that will smooth the way to your combined future.

A SIMPLE TASK

Take a sheet of paper and divide it into three columns. Headline each: Past, Present, and Future. Then write down the one or two key issues that worry you financially in each category. For example in the "past" column you might write: protection of ownership in an existing home, or ownership in a family-owned business. In the "present" column, you might be concerned about dealing with financial issues like child support from a previous marriage, or the amount each will contribute to regular monthly expenses. And in the "future" column, your concern might be about division of property acquired during the marriage, or support for one who might give up a profession or move to a new location, impacting earnings power.

Now that you understand your financial concerns, you're ready to start planning to deal with them.

Chapter 12:

FINANCIAL BALANCING SCENARIOS

It may be easier than you think to create a financial plan that is fair and balanced in case your relationship terminates. The balancing act might require purchasing life insurance, setting up annuities, creating trusts, or changing beneficiaries on your retirement accounts or life insurance. Court-ordered maintenance is likely to be the starting point for distributing ongoing income if that is an issue. But a division of assets, and distribution of those assets, is the basic purpose of this agreement.

Since every relationship is different, let's divide the universe of couples into some typical situations. You might find ideas for your planning in one of these scenarios, even though you don't exactly fit them.

These are creative solutions, not a complete prescription, because every situation is different. And remember, while the goal is a financial solution, you're dealing with two commodities that are impossible to value in terms of money: time and emotion. Figuring out fairness is always your goal.

FIRST MARRIAGE FOR BOTH

You've had "the talk," and have some insight into each other's money attitudes as a result of doing the work at the end of chapter 3. This is a first marriage, and the glow of the engagement is bright. The last thing you want to do is make a prenuptial, but you're over that debate and have chosen your attorneys. And you've read our advice to control the process.

The first piece of advice is: decide together what you think should go into your agreement, whether financial issues or other aspects of your life together. Make a joint list of the things you want included in your agreement and then bring it separately to your attorneys. They'll certainly have suggestions. Listen carefully to them.

Make sure you cover some of the key financial issues:

In case of divorce with no children, what do you agree upon regarding support for one party or the other—during the proceedings and after the divorce is finalized?

If you leave that issue to a judge, you may not like the results. Some judges award maintenance for only one-third or half the length of the marriage. However, if incomes are equal and neither party has given up a career or relocated, the judge may not award maintenance. And, once awarded, a judge may order a future review of that maintenance to see if circumstances have changed.

Solution: The first question is whether you agree that one of you would receive support at all, based on the length of the marriage or career disruption. Then, agree to take your income figures, plus each other's retirement contributions, from the last year's tax return before a divorce, as a starting point. You could create a percentage formula where the higher-earning spouse contributes to the income for the other, but for only a limited time period, perhaps three years.

But if one party is just starting out on a career, and has been supported through professional school (medical school, law school) by the other party, then a mathematical formula based on past earnings is not enough. Future earnings must be taken into consideration.

For tax reasons, it is often better to transform ongoing maintenance obligations into a lump sum distribution of marital assets. Then something called *present value* calculations comes into play to determine what immediate lump sum is equivalent to a future stream of earnings. It's similar to winning the lottery and being given a choice between taking a smaller but immediate lump sum or a payout over your lifetime.

Sure, this sounds complicated, but if you've already discussed your household budgeting plan, it should be easy to translate that very positive agreement into a support plan in case of divorce.

In case of divorce, how will you divide personal property that you purchased together?

Solution: For personal property, agree that if you separate, you'll make a list and take turns choosing items to keep. And you can also agree that if you are keeping separate spending accounts that are not marital property, then assets purchased from those accounts remain the property of the buyer.

Will you file taxes jointly or separately?

THE NEW LOVE DEAL

This is an interesting and not idle question. It's likely that your tax bill will be higher if you are married filing separately than if you file a joint return. (And either way is likely to be higher than if you were single, although there have been attempts to erase the "marriage penalty.")

Solution: If one spouse receives taxable income from nonmarital property or otherwise generates more income from work or investments, you could certainly file jointly, but agree that the spouse whose assets or income generated the disproportionate tax is responsible for paying that extra tax—or at least a larger portion of the tax, depending on whether the assets and income are being used for their mutual benefit.

You might choose to file separately if one of you has complicated, ongoing business interests that might invite scrutiny from the IRS. The slightly higher tax bill might be worth avoiding the costs of dealing with tax attorneys and submitting to audits. (Of course, if you're really worried about signing a joint return, you might want to reconsider signing the marriage license!)

If you're really worried about signing a joint return, you might want to reconsider signing the marriage license!)

Who will save for retirement, now that you're a couple?

Solution: That's an easy answer. Each of you will save individually for retirement, although you may decide to agree on a certain amount for each. You never know what circumstances will change in the next forty or more years, which is why retirement accounts are named individually. Each of you should make a contribution to the retirement plan at work or an individual retirement account. And remember, even a nonworking spouse is entitled to contribute to an IRA—$5,000 or $6,000 if you're age fifty or older. If you agree, your prenuptial could specify that these are off-limits for consideration in the event of a divorce.

But be warned that in many states pension benefits and even retirement savings may be considered as part of the marital estate, unless specifically excluded in your agreement. That means a court would issue a qualified domestic relations order (QDRO) to separate a portion of one spouse's retirement benefits in case of divorce. And state law may require an equalization of retirement benefits, depending on the length of the marriage.

These issues apply to almost every couple. Talking about what really matters to you is not a sign of mistrust—it is a sign of trust. Writing down those things you are willing to do and hope to accomplish is not selfish—it is the essence of commitment. That's the basis for your New Love Deal.

Writing down those things you are willing to do and hope to accomplish is not selfish—it is the essence of commitment.

But many couples come together with specific needs and circumstances, based on age, marital history, unequal wealth, and ongoing financial responsibilities to others. Here are a few creative ways to deal with those issues. See where you might fit in.

ANY AGE COUPLE, SUBSTANTIAL ASSETS OWNED BY EACH

Many couples come into a marriage with significant individual assets. Both may have careers and high incomes, as well as their own property. That creates a separate set of issues. Whether it is a first marriage or a subsequent marriage, how do you fairly structure a division of assets that might occur in case of divorce or death?

Solution: Start by each creating a separate revocable living trust (RLT) to hold title to assets that are brought into the marriage and are intended to be kept separate in case of death or divorce. An RLT is simply a trust you create while you are alive and that you manage at your discretion.

You must officially change the title on your assets—house, mutual fund, stocks, bank account, property—from your own name, Susan Smith, to the Susan Smith Revocable Living Trust. There are no tax implications for this change, and you can still buy and sell property and pay applicable taxes on your personal tax return.

At your death, the successor trustee you have named will take over the trust and distribute the assets as you have legally directed—without going through the time-consuming and expensive process of probate.

Then, as part of your prenuptial agreement, you will state that in the event of death or divorce, the assets held in your own living trust will not at any time become marital assets. You may specify that even if you live in a house titled in one person's living trust or the spouse contributes to maintenance or remodeling of the house, it remains the sole property of the individual trust and not a marital asset.

A revocable living trust is such a good idea for anyone, since it organizes your assets and instructions, and is very useful if you are incapacitated (since your named successor trustee can take over the responsibilities without a court order). So, in addition to your individual RLTs, you might want to create an additional, joint RLT to hold the marital assets you will build up together—joint savings or investment accounts, or the new home you purchase in joint name. That way, your assets will be divided neatly into premarital and marital assets. And the assets will be far easier to divide if you want to undo your deal.

What if one of you has an expensive or lingering illness and uses up a substantial portion of the marital assets?

Solution: This is an issue that could affect all marriages, no matter what the age or financial situation of the couple. Health insurance does not cover the cost of custodial care, and it can be very expensive. That kind of care is not just for older people; think of the cost of care for Superman, Christopher Reeve, when he was paralyzed in an accident.

The solution is for the couple to purchase long-term care insurance

The solution is for the couple to purchase long-term care insurance, which pays the cost of custodial care either at home, in assisted living, or in a nursing home if that becomes necessary. There is a discount for spouses on most policies. The time to buy is when you're healthy and in your fifties, but it is available into your seventies—if you qualify. You'll want coverage of at least $200 per day, plus an inflation protection.

Or you could purchase a combination life/long-term care policy, so if the money is not used for care, the beneficiary receives a death benefit. For more information, there are four chapters on the subject of long-term care insurance in *The Savage Truth on Money* and searchable in Terry's columns posted at www.TerrySavage.com.

SECOND MARRIAGE WITH MINOR CHILDREN INVOLVED

One or both of you will have ongoing responsibilities, both financial and parental, to a child who may or may not live with you. If money is a huge cause of divorce in second marriages, children from a previous relationship are a close second. You have some things to discuss—and some possible solutions.

If one of you has a financial obligation for child support and the other does not, and therefore has more money to save, should a marital split require an equal division of savings that were built up by the parent who did not pay ongoing support?

Solution: Keep track of the money paid out of joint accounts for child support (including gifts, clothing, college funding, and emergency money), in the case of a division of assets. Then that amount can be credited to the nonparent partner in any future division of assets. That way, the nonparent partner is not subsidizing the child-support obligation.

How do you deal with college savings for children from this, and previous, marriages?

If college for the child of a previous marriage is a legal obligation, how will it be balanced by the need to save for college for the children of this marriage—either during the marriage or in case of divorce?

Solution: Open a 529 college savings account for each child, and fund them equally every year. That money will grow automatically tax-free, for use for college expenses. (For more information on 529 college savings plans, go to www.SavingforCollege.com.) In addition, the parent could take out life insurance policies, naming each child (and a trustee for the child if a minor) as beneficiary. That would provide money for college. Premium payments for this policy for children from a prior marriage would be an obligation of the parent, not the couple, and should come from the parent's premarital or separate assets.

SECOND MARRIAGE WITH ADULT CHILDREN INVOLVED

Your adult children may want you to be happy, but you shouldn't be surprised to realize that they are equally interested in their own financial future. If you announce you're remarrying, you'll learn a lot about their motivation. But sometimes, the kids have it right. They worry not so much about your use of "their inheritance" while you are alive and in control, but what happens in case of a divorce or death. Those are realistic issues to plan

If you announce you're remarrying, you'll learn a lot about their motivation. But sometimes, the kids have it right.

139

for, and they'll be relieved in either case that you've consulted your attorneys. Don't take offense; take action.

How do you deal with your adult children from previous marriages, who are worried about you, and your assets?

Solution: The easiest way to deal with this issue—if you qualify based on your health—is to purchase cash-value life insurance with your children (or a trust) as the policy owners and beneficiaries. Then you can gift money to the children or the trustees of your irrevocable insurance trust, giving enough money each year to pay the insurance premium. That death benefit will replace the assets you intend to leave to your new spouse—and since the policy is not owned by you, it won't be considered part of your estate.

You'll likely want to explain this provision fully to your adult children, since they will be receiving the money (or will be trustees of the trust that receives the money) to pay the life insurance premiums. Explain to them that the proceeds of the life insurance policy are intended to equalize their share of the estate with your new spouse, so that all are appropriately benefited. Knowledge of these arrangements can smooth family resentments of your new marriage.

To avoid problems, should I distribute my estate to my children before I remarry?

Solution: That's a bad idea for several reasons. Your attorney can explain more fully how to use sophisticated estate-planning techniques. But by distributing more than the allowed amount (currently $14,000 per year, per person), you are subject to the current combined estate and gift tax rules. And the real reason not to give away money to avoid family fights is you might need it!

One more solution is to create an estate plan that provides for separate trusts, both to take advantage of tax laws and to provide income for a current spouse, while leaving assets to surviving children. A word of warning: don't create an estate plan that requires adult children to wait for the passing of the current spouse before they can receive any of their inheritance. You want your adult children to receive their intended share of your estate upon your death—*not* having to wait until the death of your new spouse. That's a negative approach that's bound to build ill will. (Please note other estate-planning tips near the end of this chapter.)

ANY AGE COUPLE WITH WIDELY DIFFERENT FINANCIAL STATUSES

This is the typical scenario most people think of when the word prenup surfaces. Think Donald Trump, or Rupert Murdock, or Sandra Bullock. It may be either a wealthy man or woman who wants protection and thinks it is especially important when the financial situations of the parties are wildly different.

A prenup, structured correctly, can be an advantage to both. The wealthier person knows how the marriage will end financially, limiting ongoing concerns about future division of property and allowing the focus to be on building a life together. The less advantaged person knows he or she has a certain amount of future financial security, alleviating worries about what will happen to the relationship. As you go through this process, it's important to warn the person with fewer assets not to allow him- or herself to be undervalued and unprotected. Remember that you may become so accustomed to a certain lifestyle that you need to be able to afford it if you are on your own.

A prenup, structured correctly, can be an advantage to both

In other words, as you negotiate this agreement—whether you are a man or a woman—don't be so afraid to be labeled a "gold digger" that you undervalue one of the very reasons your fiancé wants to marry you. Romantic? Hardly. Realistic? Absolutely!

Here are some possible solutions, especially useful if this marriage beats all expectations and lasts for many years. Is it fair to stick to the original, agreed-upon division of assets at death or divorce?

Solution: Structure the prenup much as an old-fashioned pension plan, which used to reward employees for longevity through a process called vesting. For example, the agreement could say that a certain amount of assets will be provided in settlement if the marriage lasts perhaps one year and an increasing amount for every year thereafter.

Or this same agreement could be structured in percentage terms—with percentages of income or income and assets to be divided on a scaled basis if the marriage lasts to a certain point.

For example, you could agree that if the marriage lasts longer than one year, the spouse who earns less will get 10 percent of the marital assets, 20 percent for additional years, and so on until one spouse gets half of the assets accumulated in the marriage after being married for five or seven years.

ANY AGE COUPLE WITH RESPONSIBILITIES FROM A PREVIOUS MARRIAGE

The past is past—until it collides with the present. I'd advise any prospective couple to share the terms of their previous divorce agreements. Yes, much is agreed to under pressure, and a lot of rhetoric fills the settlement papers, but after all, when your now fiancé(e) was previously married, he or she professed eternal love to that spouse. Much more than curiosity is involved. As the next spouse, you might be "inheriting" some heavy financial obligations. And you're getting a good insight into how well your new spouse lives up to his or her commitments.

The past is past—until it collides with the present.

What are the ongoing support, insurance, and other financial requirements of a prior divorce, and how will they impact your new marital property?

Solution: Have an honest discussion about which account the payments will be drawn upon. The payments should be made from separate assets or should come from income before any contribution to a joint expense account. Otherwise, the new spouse will be angry at "supporting" her or his predecessor. If the amount will impact your future lifestyle together, it's wise to fully disclose the specifics of this obligation.

ANY AGE COUPLE, LIVING IN HIS OR HER HOUSE

Here's a common situation that can be tricky. You decide to live in the house that your spouse already owns. You're not afraid of "ghosts" of spouses past. But you do need to do some planning for the future.

What happens if the spouse that owns the house dies, and wants the new spouse to continue living there, but the home is a large portion of the estate designated for the children of the first marriage?

Solution: As part of your prenuptial agreement, you can specify a *life estate*, or a fixed period of time that your spouse can remain in the house. Or you can leave the home to your spouse, if your children have no particular use for it. Then, take out a life insurance policy on your life, owned by your children, who are also the beneficiaries. That death benefit will offset the value of the house, which will now go to your surviving spouse.

COUPLE WITH A WIDE AGE DIFFERENTIAL

We know too many happy couples to presume that an age difference precludes a happy marriage. But you don't have to be a Las Vegas oddsmaker to bet that the older spouse will die first. And that creates some interesting problems—especially if there are children or grandchildren from a previous marriage. Once again, a prenuptial agreement dealing with these issues must be linked with a sophisticated estate plan.

What happens to all the money when she or he dies? Consider the situation of Anna Nicole Smith. Oops, too late. But you know her story: the survivor often has to fight for her or his share of the estate in court against other family members who can't believe Mom or Dad wasn't unduly influenced.

Solution: In this case, a prenuptial agreement that is tied to an estate plan helps substantiate the wishes of the older spouse regarding his or her estate. An estate-planning attorney will recommend clauses against challenging the provisions of the will or trust. For example, a clause could say that any challenge to the estate plan will completely disinherit the challenger. Setting aside money for children or grandchildren in specially created trusts also demonstrates the purpose of the plan.

What if the younger spouse is only involved for the money? That's the question that might be on the mind of all interested parties—including the older spouse. They say there's no fool like an old fool. But instead of breaking up the relationship, a good agreement can legitimize those concerns.

What if the younger spouse is only involved for the money?

Solution: This is where the prenup agreement can cover issues that relate to division of assets not only in case of divorce, but also in case of death or a lingering illness. And certainly, this situation calls for an estate-planning attorney to coordinate with the provisions of the prenup. Some agreements have specified that the younger spouse must be living with and caring for the older spouse to receive a full distribution of benefits. On the other hand, there have been many younger spouses who have served as caretakers for a much-loved spouse, only to find that the estate plan did not in any way compensate the caregiver, not only for time, but also for earnings that were forgone.

Discussing death and caregiving roles is critical in a prenup where the age difference is significant. To avoid that under the guise of "true love" is to bet against the odds—too often a losing proposition.

ONE HAS INHERITED MONEY

As long as an inheritance is kept separate, it is not a marital asset. But it could have a bearing on the couple's lifestyle—and the award that might be given in divorce court absent a prenuptial agreement. For example, income from inherited assets is considered income for child support. And if the income is used to maintain a couple's lifestyle, a judge might consider it in awarding maintenance.

Once again, disclosure and separation of assets—both before and after marriage—are critical elements in dealing with this situation. And you'll need to include specific language in your agreement to deal with these issues.

How do I keep my inheritance separate while using some of the money to sustain our lifestyle?

Solution: If your parents had good estate planning, their bequest to you was set up in a trust created by the estate. Keep all assets titled in that trust, and do not use any of the trust proceeds to buy assets in joint name. Do not name your spouse as a trustee of that inherited trust. Insert a clause in your agreement that any benefits flowing from the trust and used to support your lifestyle are not considered marital assets for purposes of dissolution of the marriage. If you received your inheritance directly, and not within a trust, set up your own trust to hold the money and assets you received as an inheritance. Then, follow the same procedures about keeping both the principal and income separate from your marital assets.

SENIORS WORRIED ABOUT LOSING BENEFITS IF MARRIED

Many benefits afforded to seniors—from Social Security to Medicare and long-term nursing care—have income limits that could be exceeded when two seniors marry. It's sad but true that many seniors must do these calculations before

It's sad but true that many seniors must do these calculations before even moving in together.

even moving in together. Instead of a prenuptial agreement, a cohabitation agreement similar to the one described above, as well as a health-care power of attorney, revocable living trust, and living will should be created.

One area that is critical to consider is the spousal exemption for assets, which is different in each state, if one of the couple must turn to Medicaid for nursing home care. A home in which a spouse still lives is often exempt from state spend-down provisions, which require near-impoverishment to qualify for Medicaid. But if you are not married, living in a home owned by the person entering a state-funded nursing home, it is likely that the property must be sold. This is also an important issue in financial planning for same-sex couples who are not married. The solution is to consider purchase of long-term care insurance, so you will not be dependent on state aid.

Senior Solutions

Many financial issues arise that are specific to seniors. The two greatest are the cost of long-term care and the issue of "running out of money."

Solution: Long-term care (LTC) insurance. The issue of the cost of care is addressed by the long-term care insurance noted earlier. Many seniors can still afford to purchase coverage in their seventies, though the policies are less expensive at a younger age. Many LTC insurers allow domestic partners to qualify for the same discounts afforded to married couples. Or, if you have savings available, you can purchase a cash-value life insurance policy that allows the cash to be accessed, and leveraged, to pay for custodial care. If the care isn't needed, the death benefit will benefit the survivor.

Solution: Reverse Mortgage. The issue of running out of money is one that most seniors face, as longevity increases and costs of medical care rise. For seniors who own their own home, a reverse mortgage can provide liquidity, while allowing the seniors to remain in their home. This is basically a tax-free withdrawal of home equity available to people over age sixty-two who have a fully paid home or only a small remaining mortgage. They can withdraw a lump sum or a check a month for life without losing control of their home. When the home is sold, either after their death or when they move out, the amounts advanced are repaid to the lender. The heirs can either refinance and keep the house or keep any additional equity when the property is sold. You, or your heirs, can never owe more than sale value of the home— even if you've withdrawn more cash over the years.

A reverse mortgage can provide liquidity, while allowing the seniors to remain in their home.

Seniors who are cohabiting must give careful thought to this prospect for increased income. If the home is titled in the name of one person, then the income will stop and the house must be sold when that person dies. If the house is in joint name, the surviving partner can remain in the home. For more information and an estimate of how much cash you could withdraw, go to www.ReverseMortgage.org.

CONCLUSION

The purpose of this chapter was to serve as a guideline to the problems that can arise and to offer potential solutions. As we note throughout the book, your situation is unique. That's why you'll have your own attorney, estate planner, and financial advisor.

If this is the moment you decide it's "way too complicated" to understand, "way too time-consuming" when you're planning a wedding, or "way too untrusting" to discuss the terms of the Love Deal with your life partner, one day you may be "way too sorry" you didn't do that written agreement. And then you'll learn how "way too expensive" divorce or separation can be!

Then you'll learn how "way too expensive" divorce or separation can be!

Having financial concerns does not diminish the importance of your relationship. But feeling insecure about voicing those concerns is an indication that you feel your relationship is not strong enough to survive an open discussion about things that are very important to you: your financial security, your children, your family, your future.

If you truly don't believe that the person you are planning to spend your future with can accept your concerns, then you might want to think twice about the foundation for this relationship. No. It won't get better with time. Each of you will be walking on eggshells, avoiding issues that can derail your life together. Do it *now*—before the costs are financial, as well as emotional.

Remember, your Love Deal is not an encouragement to failure; it is a road map to success. The less you argue about when you're happiest, the less you will disagree about during the inevitable stresses of a long relationship. That's the Savage Truth!

MAKE A LIST OF SIGNIFICANT FINANCIAL CONCERNS

Your task at the end of this chapter is to review the scenarios, consider your own issues—and each make a list. There may be only one or two financial concerns to be discussed. And they may require the help of a financial planner to come up with appropriate solutions. But you won't be able to resolve these concerns if you aren't willing to admit to them. You decide whether this is best done over a glass of wine or a cup of coffee. Just prepare to be as emotionally generous with your partner as you would wish him or her to be with you.

Now, each of you should get started on making that list!

Chapter 13:

DEAL-MAKING TIPS

When you make a prenuptial agreement or cohabitation plan, you're venturing into the world of attorneys and financial advisors. It's complicated, and that's why you each need your own attorney. But the advice can be overwhelming, especially when it comes to financial planning.

So, here are a few "Terry's Tips"—things to consider and questions to ask, before signing either the prenuptial agreement or the new estate plan, will, and revocable living trust that typically go along with a prenup. Talking about what really matters to you is not a sign of mistrust—it is a sign of trust. Writing down those things you are willing to do and hope to accomplish is not selfish—it is the essence of commitment. That's the basis for your New Love Deal.

And after those tips, I'll include some advice for parents, and some next steps to make sure your agreement works as planned.

OWN THE LIFE INSURANCE POLICY

If you're the person designated to be the beneficiary (the one who gets paid) of a life insurance policy, you should make sure that in addition to being named beneficiary, you are also the *owner* of the policy. The policy owner can change beneficiaries at any time and can stop paying premiums. If you're just the beneficiary, you might never know when the insurance policy lapses!

If you're just the beneficiary, you might never know when the insurance policy lapses!

Solution: In cases of life insurance ordered as part of a divorce settlement, if you want to make sure the policy stays paid and in force and that you are still the beneficiary, you should arrange for your ex-spouse to send the annual premium payments to you or directly to the insurance company, where—as policy owner—you have the right to check that the payment was made.

MAKE THE SMART ASSET CHOICE

When marital assets are divided, frequently the custodial parent gets the house, in order to continue the routines of child rearing. At the same time, the other spouse gets the retirement account. Bad deal! There's no way of knowing whether the house will ever appreciate, but it's certain that property taxes will rise and the roof or something else will need repair. Meanwhile, the retirement account is likely to continue growing tax-deferred.

Solution: Where substantial assets are involved, seek the advice of a financial advisor. A nonworking spouse especially should demand a share of any retirement accounts, and make sure that a qualified domestic relations order (QDRO) is served on the company retirement plan or retirement account trustee, dividing the funds as ordered. (The money may continue to grow tax-deferred until the worker retires, but in separate "buckets.")

The house may continue to be a shared asset, to be sold after the children are in college. And there should be agreement that insurance, property taxes, and maintenance expenses remain a joint liability. Given the recent volatility of real estate markets, the wealthier spouse may give a guarantee of the minimum amount that the other spouse will receive.

FUND AGREEMENTS SECURELY

The courts are filled with former spouses seeking to hold their previous mates to financial agreements. Entrepreneurs can hide income and assets. Employees can lose jobs. Any agreement to pay in the future is only as secure as the commitment of the person to make the promised payments. And this promise comes from the person you are divorcing! Plan for this in advance as part of your prenuptial agreement, which should say that any payment must be securely funded.

Solution: Have your prenup state that at least a portion of any payout agreement will be funded with an annuity. This is an insurance contract that will pay a fixed amount for life—sort of like taking a lotto payout over your lifetime. A lump sum today will become a monthly check forever. Go to www.immediateannuities.com to see how much money it will take to fund an immediate lifetime annuity in a specific amount for a person at any given age. Always remember, though, that over time inflation will erode the purchasing power of that fixed monthly check.

BE VIGILANT IN ESTATE PLANNING

Under current estate tax laws, spouses can leave an unlimited amount of property or other assets to each other upon death, with no estate tax owed. The problem arises when the second spouse dies—and then the taxman comes with a vengeance because the combined estate may trigger a substantial estate tax. (Remember, your estate includes the value of your home, retirement plans, and even life insurance if you own the policy, so your estate can add up quickly as you grow older.)

There is a frequently used technique to reduce this estate tax burden. Instead of leaving everything outright to the surviving spouse, the estate-planning attorneys set up a separate *bypass trust*. An amount equal to the estate tax exemption (currently $5.25 million) is left to this bypass trust to take advantage of the tax benefits. Then, the remainder could pass tax-free to the spouse. (Of course, cohabiting couples or those in civil unions do not receive this federal estate tax benefit.) And despite the Supreme Court ruling, while this exemption is likely to apply to federal estate taxes, the state may apply its own laws, and not recognize the exemption for state tax purposes.

Warning: Often, estate-planning attorneys set up unnecessarily restrictive trusts, which do not give the surviving spouse flexibility to deal with the money received in trust. Although the money is "promised" to the surviving spouse, she or he will later find out that she or he cannot withdraw money without permission of the trustees, cannot change the terms of the distribution of the remaining money after her or his own death, and cannot change the investment advisors to the trust.

Solution: Attend the meetings with the estate-planning attorney. Always ask these simple questions: "If my spouse dies, what assets come directly to me? Is there any restriction on my ability to withdraw, invest, or bequest that money upon my death?"

And, just to make sure, before signing a complicated estate-planning document with significant assets involved, request a copy of the plan—and pay an independent attorney to review it before you sign.

TILL DEATH DO US PART – THE REST OF THE DEAL

Whether you're married, living together, or single, you definitely need an estate plan. Don't worry if you don't have much in the way of money or assets. You might use your Love Deal attorney to draw up your new will or a revocable living trust described here so that the documents are coordinated.

Even if you just name each other as a beneficiary or hold assets in joint name, you need an estate plan. Those documents will give instructions about nonmonetary things, such as your wishes for funeral plans and custody of your minor children. Absent other instructions, simultaneous deaths in an accident could have your families fighting over many of these issues.

Since your estate plan—the one each of you will create—must follow the terms of your prenup, you might as well get it all done at the same time. If you're dealing with a large law firm, they likely have an estate-planning attorney who will draw up the documents. Maybe you'll even get a discount for all the legal work you're giving the firm!

An estate plan or will is not a do-it-yourself project. If there's a mistake, you won't be around to fix it by the time it's discovered.

But don't procrastinate. And an estate plan or will is not a do-it-yourself project. If there's a mistake, you won't be around to fix it by the time it's discovered.

DON'T FORGET TO CHANGE BENEFICIARIES

You may want to name your new spouse or partner as your beneficiary on your retirement plans or life insurance policies. Remember, these assets pass directly to the heirs you have named, regardless of your will or estate plan.

Similarly, if you intend to hold assets jointly, you might need to change the title to a house that one of you owns. Ask your accountant about any tax consequences of such a transfer.

Even better than joint tenancy, you might want to create a joint revocable living trust to hold title to property that you will share equally. This trust will ensure that if either of you is incapacitated, the other can act without requiring court approval.

Yes, we know you're thinking about marriage or living together—not death. But we're very superstitious. Any planning left undone is an invitation to disaster. Now that you're going to be a couple, you need to handle all the legalities.

But we're very superstitious. Any planning left undone is an invitation to disaster.

156

Follow Through on Your Deal

Once your Love Deal is executed, each party is to use good faith in following through on what you agreed to, including making whatever dispositions you agreed to make in your will. The interaction can get more complex with trusts and complicated assets, though, so the best rule is a regular "legal checkup," where you check in with your respective attorneys every couple of years to see if the agreement or your estate planning needs a tune-up to conform to your original plans and promises.

Creating your deal is a process, not a moment in time. Although you will each sign off on your deal, you will each live with it—and its opportunities as well as its limitations. The deal comes at the start of your combined lives, and if it is done well, it will have room to breathe and grow, creating your foundation for a strong life together.

Your Immediate Tasks

- Get out your current will or estate plan (if you have one) and review its provisions.

- Make a list of all accounts that require designated beneficiaries, including life insurance, retirement plans, savings bonds, and some bank accounts. Changing beneficiaries does not require an attorney, only written notification to the custodian company.

- Check on ownership of life insurance policies. Your agreement may require the creation of an irrevocable life insurance trust to own newly purchased policies that fund your agreement.

- Take your completed prenup agreement to your estate-planning attorney (or separate attorneys) to make sure your new estate documents coordinate with your agreement.

Chapter 14:

DON'T COURT DISASTER

What happens if you don't follow our advice in creating your New Love Deal? Can you afford to ignore our suggestions, ideas, and warnings? Maybe you will sail smoothly into happily ever after. Or maybe you will become part of that tidal wave that engulfs the divorce courts and makes divorce so costly.

If you can't work out your deal now, while you are most in love and in harmony, what will it look like when you engage battling attorneys to fight on your behalf in court? Can you expect a better or less expensive result in court? And can you count on the courts to act like Solomon and divide your fortune, and your emotions, with fairness and respect?

Michele, a divorce court judge for nineteen years before becoming a

If you can't work out your deal now, while you are most in love and in harmony, what will it look like when you engage battling attorneys to fight on your behalf in court?

professional mediator, has a unique perspective. And she was gracious enough to let us include some material from her best-selling book, *The Good Karma Divorce* (HarperCollins, 2010). So now, hear from the judge.

When I wrote *The Good Karma Divorce*, I devoted a lot of time and attention to the misperceptions of the court process. We all have heard horrific stories about people who go through the divorce process – stories about the courts, the lawyers, and the judges. But by and large that doesn't seem to penetrate those in a state of optimism. It is not my intention to ambush that state. However, I want you to think about what really happens in the divorcing process. Think about this in the same disciplined way that you would review facts about smoking or spending too much time in the sun without protection.

My intention is to give you the highest level of outcome whether your relationship sustains or it doesn't. Given the current reality, the idea of not preparing for an alternate outcome really does not make sense. Even though our wisdom clearly tells us that people are damaged in the adversarial process, there is still a blind spot. And because the cause and effect are so far in the future, the effect of having no contract is really hard to grasp. But unlike a pharmaceutical side effect, the risk of personal damage from a breakup can really be minimized in a document.

Why so many put their head in the sand about the value of prenups

Why so many put their head in the sand about the value of prenups and relationship contracts has been a penetrating question for me since they first handed me the gavel and robe.

and relationship contracts has been a penetrating question for me since they first handed me the gavel and robe. Eventually I realized that it wasn't that people just put their heads in the sand about the possibility of breakup, but they had a fantasy about being protected by the system in the event there was a breakup. Therefore, when considering whether to contract or not to contract, it is crucial that I address any misconceptions you might have about the divorce and breakup process in the courts.

The breakup process is so jagged and unpredictable, and people are raw, frightened, and bewildered. It is hard to imagine that given this complexity a court of law can be the best to design the fate of families. Now you have an opportunity to design your own fate.

The prenuptial agreement is sort of a promissory note that people make to each other that in the event of devastation they will attempt compassion and civility. Or you can think of it as an insurance policy against our random, chaotic, and turbulent times.

For nineteen years as a judge, I have watched the results for families who had the foresight to enter into prenuptial agreements and the ones that didn't. I am not advising you consider this just because it's practical or smart, but because I know in fact what happens when there isn't an agreement, especially when there are assets to fight over.

Yes, it is true that life is a hard teacher, because first you get the test, then you get the lesson. My question to you is why not minimize the harshness of the test and the lesson? That's what the New Love Deal is all about.

Yes, it is true that life is a hard teacher, because first you get the test, then you get the lesson.

There is a culturally pervasive view that the willingness to engage in a court fight signifies strength or a show of resolve. My observation is that people often choose to let the courts resolve their differences when they need to feel powerful in a dispute.

Preparing for trial requires superhuman strength. Many people try to simultaneously mobilize sufficient reserves of the required negative emotion while trying to remain on moral high ground. An angry confrontation can alter the course of negotiations and with the flick of a switch lead a lost couple into a nasty divorce.

ORDER IN THE COURT COULD RESULT IN DISORDER IN YOUR LIFE

"How did I get here?" you ask yourself. "I had no choice. I had no options," you say. But it is not really as simple as that. When you find yourself at the end of your marital journey, it is excruciating to witness the brutality in the spouse you once loved, and to have a glimpse of your own brutal nature. You have shocked yourself with how easily, and even candidly, you revealed your spouse's personal secrets to your attorney and then published those private embarrassments in a public court record. There are rare exceptions, but in order to find yourself in court, you have almost certainly had to align yourself with negative and often erroneous assumptions.

TEN DETRIMENTAL MISCONCEPTIONS ABOUT WHAT REALLY HAPPENS IN COURT

So, lest you think that creating your Love Deal is too expensive, too potentially dangerous, and totally unnecessary, let me intrude with a judge's view of reality. Here are ten of the most misguided and, therefore, harmful misconceptions about divorce, followed by some helpful truths.

1. Destruction of your spouse is an acceptable means for getting what you need.

2. Your goals can be accomplished and sure victory attained by putting on a good fight. However, unlike traditional battle, where you can destroy and walk away, you might have to deal with your adversary for years to come.

3. Once you ignite a match in the courtroom, you can control the direction and intensity of the flames.

4. Your attorney will understand and execute your goals and desires in a way that satisfies your sensitivities and needs.

5. Your concept of fairness will approximate that of the judge's. You believe there is a clear-cut, nondiscretionary standard of justice that is not dependent upon the judge's personal values.

6. Your habitual negative thought patterns, fueled by well-developed propaganda to "create the enemy," will cease once the trial is over.

7. It is your spouse's fault you are at trial.

8. The judge wields a wand, not a gavel, and can magically solve your problems, no matter how much damage has been done to the family.

9. The court process will not hurt you, because you are invulnerable. In any case, whatever pain you feel will go away once the trial is over.

10. Your attorney can be vicious to your spouse, because that is your attorney's conduct, not yours. And people who are abusively cross-examined in court never hold it against their spouse.

TEN TRUTHS TO DILUTE SOME OF YOUR MISCONCEPTIONS

1. Winning is not necessarily a matter of being stronger or more effective, as it is in real battle, because the outcome is decided by a judge who will have only a snapshot of who you are or may not see your position the way you do.

2. You can rehearse your testimony until you have achieved perfection, but you have no way of knowing how you will be perceived on the witness stand. How well do you know yourself? Can you know how you will react when you are in an unfamiliar, pressure-cooker situation without any experience to guide you? I have seen the tightest cases fall apart when a testifier gets what I call "witness fever." Witness fever happens when the testifier has the irresistible urge to ad-lib testimony and discards the script.

3. The judge might ask an unexpected question that puts a stiletto directly into the soft spot of your case.

Unexpected truths that you had never contemplated rise to the surface.

4. If you are going to trial on principle and are seeking to vindicate some moral standard that is crucial to you, you should know that moral standards and principles are not what courts are meant to address. Trials only address the law. For example, in a no-fault state, adultery is not relevant.

5. In your struggle for dominance over your spouse or the dominance of your legal position, you relinquish all control over your own familial and financial life. Ultimately you have no control over the outcome of your case. Unlike an architect, guided by a blueprint, a court battle is unpredictable. Court battles are laden with information that is not true and theories that do not hold up, while exhaustion and fear can color decisions you or your attorney must make in an instant.

. Court battles are laden with information that is not true and theories that do not hold up,

6. Even in no-fault states, the courts are sensitive to helping victims and are sometimes punitive toward perpetrators of harm to a spouse or children. Attorneys know this. Attorneys might upgrade the decibels of the negative behavior or put a twisted spin on innocent behavior. A father had thrown the bat down after

he struck out at a father-son Little League game; by the time the parties went to trial, the story turned into the father tried to hit his son with the bat. The fruit of a hostile imagination about your spouse is at its ripest in court and takes the form of character assassination. Don't forget that your children may someday be able to get transcripts of the hearing.

7. Even under oath some people may lie. I have seen people lie about small things; one husband lied about throwing out his wife's favorite shoes. The tiniest lie, once revealed, can completely ruin credibility. Many a well-rehearsed witness who is usually honest can be infected by the nervous dread of being caught in a small lie. The $500 you have in your sock drawer and didn't disclose, if revealed at trial, could destroy your case.

8. Ultimately you will have to take responsibility for your part of the hostilities you have set in motion in court. People love to come up to me at parties and tell me how the system ripped them off. By scapegoating we transfer some of our own responsibility onto the adversarial process. The court process is far from perfect, but not accepting your own responsibility will further entrench a victim mind-set.

9. Moving forward with your life is critical to the process of healing. A court battle requires freezing at the stage of blame and fault. The debate escalates in court, focusing on who did what to whom. Character maligning becomes the focus rather than problem-solving. This has an effect on you (and your relationship with your former spouse) that will last well beyond the end

of the trial. Many people have told me years later that they wished they had never gone to trial because of how much it hurt them and their family.

10. The majority of cases that go to trial are not about the financial bottom line, but about an emotional attachment to a perceived righteous position. This attachment blocks the clarity that would allow a vision of the bigger picture. Too often, people end up in trial because they can't tolerate any more negotiations. You think you are at the end of your collective ability to problem-solve. But that is not true. You may not really be at a stalemate; you may just have stale negotiations.

The majority of cases that go to trial are not about the financial bottom line, but about an emotional attachment to a perceived righteous position.

Why We Care

The three of us debated whether this chapter was necessary, or too much of a downer. After all, we're trying to help you create a harmonious relationship in order to avoid just this kind of scenario. But if you haven't been in divorce court—either as a participant or as a friend—it is hard to imagine how acrimonious a battle with no predetermined agreement can be.

If you think this chapter was painful to read, just imagine how painful it would be to live through the process of a divorce battle in court, or even a civil lawsuit at the end of a live-in relationship. This pain rings a bell, because we each know someone who has been through the process and, no matter what the financial settlement, came out the worse for the wear.

It is exactly this type of breakup that lovers hope to avoid by not thinking about it. But Scarlett O'Hara's mantra of "I'll think about it tomorrow" is not the solution for avoiding a bitter battle. Far better to plan ahead, when your relationship is strong, your motives are the best, and the lawyers are far more inclined to follow your directives to compromise to reach agreement.

If you think this chapter was painful to read, just imagine how painful it would be to live through the process of a divorce battle in court, or even a civil lawsuit at the end of a live-in relationship

Chapter 15:

A POSTSCRIPT ON POSTNUPS

Those who are already married or in a committed relationship may realize that their prenuptial agreement needs recalibrating—or that their relationship does.

Fortunately, there is a document that married couples can create during their marriage that is a tool in the arsenal of maintaining satisfying marriages. Commonly called a postnuptial agreement, this tool can be used in two interesting situations: when an unexpected change of circumstances has occurred, or problems are erupting that threaten to erode the personal bond.

In both cases, each party needs a lawyer. In the past, it was assumed that a husband and wife could not contract with each other because the husband would be able to exert pressure and influence over the wife. In this unequal bargaining position, it was feared that the wife would be compelled to give up rights and assets. In the courts today, there are still remnants of this suspicion, and the courts look even more closely at making sure there was proper legal representation for postnups. Talking about what really matters to you is not a sign of mistrust—it is a sign of trust. Writing down those things you are willing to do and hope to accomplish is not selfish—it is the essence of commitment. That's the basis for your New Love Deal.

Similar to prenups, a postnup must include full disclosure of assets, and there can be no fraud or coercion. Unlike the prenup, which may appear to be heavy-handed, with one party giving up substantial rights, a postnup must appear to be fairer. Furthermore, every state has different interpretations of the law dealing with postnups.

A postnuptial agreement must contain something called *consideration*. This means that if someone gives something up, he or she must get something. Courts look very closely at postnups to make sure that one party was not coerced into giving up something of value without receiving something in return. The interpretation of whether there was consideration is a difficult concept even for the courts.

Two Examples

A state court felt it was valid consideration when a wife agreed to end the separation from her husband if he promised to pay her a certain sum of money should he become drunk or abuse her again. She gave something of value—agreeing not to separate—and he gave something of value—agreeing not to drink.

In a different case, a court did not believe there was sufficient consideration when a wife agreed to end their separation if the husband promised to give her half of the real estate he held prior to marriage. The court said the wife was not giving something of value, since she had no grounds for divorce.

Some attorneys hesitate to draft postnups because they may not hold up in court as readily as prenups. With the divorce rate at

50 percent of all marriages, it's quite clear that something extra is needed to save relationships in jeopardy, and a postnup might just be the answer.

Sometimes a Promise Is Not Enough

The birth of a child changes everything, from respective responsibilities to respective earnings to the spousal relationship itself. After the birth of a child, a couple falls into a new rhythm that is quite dissimilar from the original template. All the new obligations need to be addressed with conscious intent. If the parties just randomly fall into a mode of behavior, someone could easily become dissatisfied.

A friend found that she and her husband had no time for each other after the birth of their daughter. Resentment started to fester, but neither could accuse the other of wrongdoing because, after all, they were striving to improve their child's life. When they finally considered whether their relationship had to be sacrificed to be good parents, they agreed that no matter what, rain or shine, Saturday night was date night. She would slip on the high heels, and her husband would find a new restaurant and/ or show that they both could enjoy. Once they both acknowledged the importance of their relationship and went so far as to commit it to writing, they no longer had to hold tightly to their resentments.

This couple resolved their issues and stayed together, using their postnuptial agreement as a blueprint. It is worth remembering, however, that a court always has jurisdiction over the issues relating to children. That includes child support; custody; visitation; and the possible geographic restrictions on moving to another city, state, or country. The laws of your state of residence will apply in resolving these issues.

Another variable that alters the recipe for a strong marriage is a substantial change in the parties' respective income or assets. Perhaps they have shared the bill-paying equally, and now that no longer seems fair. A couple in court could not overcome their hostility for each other after the wife received a large inheritance and kept it out of the "family pot." She refused to contribute more to the bills, which was a constant source of aggravation for the husband, and like a small pebble in his shoe, it eventually threw him off balance. The wife had been hurt financially in a prior marriage, and she was unyielding on this matter. In time, they ended up divorcing.

A postnuptial agreement would have softened this problem early on if they had agreed to set aside a portion of the inheritance for the "family pot," with some of the money returned to the wife in the event of a divorce. If the above couple had objectified the problem with the assistance of a lawyer, a fair agreement could have been created. The couple could have agreed to use at least the interest on her inheritance for the family bills, or done the initial funding for a college savings plan, or any number of other good-faith gestures that would not endanger her own financial future. Without counsel as to the risk and rewards of compromises, though, most people tend to just say no. Ironically, in this case, the divorce caused everyone to be hurt financially.

Another variable is the midmarriage correction—an acknowledgment that nothing may have changed, except you or your spouse. Human relationships and individuals are forever changing, and rightfully so. Yet, it may never have occurred to a couple to enter into a prenuptial contract anticipating how they would handle inevitable changes.

A postnuptial agreement does something better than microman-age—it creates a pause in the uncoupling process you might experience as a result of increased resentment. It unifies and gives respect to each other's issues and sets an intention by the couple. They agree in writing to make certain compromise changes.

A postnuptial agreement does something better than micromanage—it creates a pause in the uncoupling process

When one or both parties agree to do something or refrain from doing something and decide to put it in writing, the parties can relax their vigilance and stop keeping score of which promises were lived up to and which were not. Cyclical, repetitive arguments can only be laid to rest once they have been dealt with. This is not to say that couples adhere completely to these contracts. But airing out an issue clearly reduces it. The couple has renegotiated their expectations. It is the unmet expectations that cause anger, disappointment, and, ultimately, resentment.

POSTNUPTIALS AS A BLUEPRINT FOR RECONCILIATION

When the parties have actually separated or are threatening to, a postnuptial agreement is an excellent blueprint for reconciliation. To commit the promises to a contract does more than say, "Okay, I promise to change. I won't run the credit cards up without us having a discussion." It is an agreement to do it with such clear intention that it is being committed to writing. Essentially, it is elevating communication, with needs articulated and formalized. Nobody has to guess what the other person really wants.

When Michele was featured as the mediator on an MSNBC documentary, *Chained to My Ex*, she arranged for an unusual agreement: the couple, remarried for the second time, was able to agree in writing that the husband would stop drinking and go to therapy with an addictions counselor or he would have to leave the marital home. For ninety days, while he got sober, the wife agreed not to bring up the husband's affair of six years ago.

With this type of clarifying communication, couples may be able to ride out a marital storm. One friend had a husband who was unfaithful during their marriage. Instead of splitting up, they worked out a written postnuptial agreement where she would receive certain of his premarital assets if he did it again. This might not work for everybody, but it worked for her. He gave attention to and dignified her needs. They have a successful marriage today.

RELATIONSHIP CHECKUPS

The dictionary defines calibration as "the act of checking or adjusting the accuracy of a measuring instrument." We calibrate, or check to ensure that the instrument has retained absolute accuracy of performance. But, as an extension of this word, we also see recalibration, and its association with marriage. That's where a postnuptial deal comes in.

A postnuptial agreement can be used to set family budgets, to determine who owns what assets, and to remove business ownership from the table in the event of divorce. They have also been used to determine how often a mother-in-law might visit or how many "boys' nights out" the husband may enjoy per month. In short, they could serve as a latter-day prenuptial agreement if "fairly" done and if local state law allows.

WHEN TO RECALIBRATE

Perhaps, an unanticipated amount of money has been spent on the children of a spouse's previous marriage. Financial issues involving children from a previous marriage are a sore spot for many couples. A friend became upset when she realized that her husband would be spending $100,000 to send his children from a former marriage to college. If they divorced, the marital estate would be worth $100,000 less. He eventually agreed to a postnup that would add $100,000 back to the marital estate if they divorced. Because of the contract, the wife felt less resentful of her husband's children, and she was willing to participate in making sure their college was paid for. She had reduced her personal risk.

Financial issues involving children from a previous marriage are a sore spot for many couples.

One spouse experiences substantial debt against her or his business that is draining on the marriage. That spouse agrees to transfer her or his interest in the real estate to the other spouse, to insulate her or him from the business debt.

A couple with a prenup has been married for ten years. One spouse says to the other, "Now that you see that this marriage is going to make it, don't you think it's time to rip up the prenup?" For a couple I know, it was actually much more than a question; the wife was starting to resent having to live under what she believed was an obsolete document that did not respect the length of the marriage or her contributions and commitment to it.

The husband was not ready to take what he considered to be a drastic step. Instead of tearing up their existing prenup, they drew up

175

a postnuptial agreement that they both could live with, by keeping some of the premarital assets protections in place and turning some of the separate assets into marital ones.

A couple moves to another state, where the laws are different, and they want to redraft their contract commensurate with the state law where they now reside. Note: if they do not create this postnuptial change, and if the original agreement specifically stated that state law would apply, then the original deal will stand.

A stay-at-home parent who has given up a career can make financial agreements to address the event of a divorce. For example, a couple might formalize a decision to give a disproportionate share of the assets to the spouse who has given up a career. The benefit is that it reduces the insecurity and resentment of the stay-at-home parent.

A couple may be impacted by a serious illness. One spouse may become a full-time caretaker, unable to pursue a career or even maintain a prior lifestyle. The one with the greater assets is often the one who is being taken care of, and the couple may desire or need to renegotiate a prenuptial agreement wherein the caretaker now receives some form of compensation. (Note: most long-term care insurance policies do not reimburse care given by a spouse.)

In essence, what a couple may need is their own "state of the union" address and subsequent written agreement in the form of a postnuptial agreement.

JUDICIAL OVERSIGHT

As these agreements involve already married parties, the courts look very closely at the bargaining dynamics and good faith of the parties. For couples, it is the process of doing a postnup that has value. It is also reassuring for couples to realize that it is a mechanism they can use if required.

However, for a judge, a postnup raises questions about the parties' motivations. How soon after the postnup did the one who benefited file for divorce? Was any leveraging done that would inhibit or create access to children?

The courts look very closely at the bargaining dynamics and good faith of the parties.

The testimony in court is scrutinized to determine if there was any undue influence. Using children is always a giveaway, since access to the children, or lack of it, is a vulnerable issue for at least one of the parties. Naturally, fear for one's physical safety would also sound an alarm.

Even though this document might ultimately be used in a divorce, a postnuptial agreement does not require or imply blame or fault of either party. A postnup only requires a sentiment that something needs to be adjusted in the marriage framework and that the couple is committed to making it better. Admitting to problems is the bridge between ending up alone and in denial and being wise enough to work things out and stay together.

POSTNUPS FOR THE UNMARRIED

Believe it or not, unmarried couples have more flexibility than do married couples when and if they choose to revise a previous agreement. Since your agreements are not tied to legal commitments, your contracts can be made anywhere and anytime. But the same principles apply—individual counsel, full disclosure, and imbalances of negotiating power will be scrutinized.

Unmarried couples must recognize that they need to be more cautious in contracting. If an agreement fails, they have no marital rights to fall back on, so they are left dependent on complicated legal theories like *unjust enrichment* or *constructive trusts*. Cohabiters should be even more acutely aware of their potential legal jeopardy without some form of a written New Love Deal.

CONCLUSION

If you've made it this far, we agree that you have changed the odds of success in your favor—whether moving in, cohabiting, creating a civil union, or getting married. While there is a huge difference in the legal recognition of those arrangements, they all have one common goal: to live together in peace, love, and harmony for the long run.

If you've made it this far, we agree that you have changed the odds of success in your favor

You would never expect to run a marathon without training, or to achieve any other personal goal without a plan. After all, a goal without a plan is just a dream! If you want to make your dreams come true, you need to do the work. And we are sure you will agree that the challenge is not too difficult if you take it step-by-step.

You may create an agreement because of specific financial needs and imbalances. Or you may create one because doing so provides a fairly regular process for getting all your cards on the table, airing your differences, and coming to agreement.

But the *worst* reason for doing an agreement is because you are under pressure! That kind of deal usually means that someone is either insecure or wants to take advantage of the moment. Ask yourself if this is the person with whom you want to enter into a long-term relationship.

PARENTAL PRESSURE

Perhaps the pressure you are feeling isn't coming from your partner, but from your own family or your partner's parents, or even from your "older but wiser" friends. In fact, you may be getting so many suggestions for your prenup that you're tempted to chuck the whole process. This is your Love Deal, so don't get upset. We have a word for your parents.

We have a word for your parents

We're assuming that many parents might choose this book and give it to their adult children who are considering living together or getting married. The sad news is you're probably too late to influence your offspring's decisions about a marriage partner. And if you approach the subject of a prenuptial agreement in the wrong way, it can certainly backfire.

Hopefully, you've instilled a sense of familial responsibility in your children, and a recognition that the work of past generations must be appropriately preserved. That doesn't preclude your son or daughter from making mistakes, but a prenuptial agreement can limit the impact of a bad decision.

If you're reading this as an adult child of wealthy parents, we advise respecting their monetary wishes—especially if they were the ones who made all the money! Consider your parents' point of view. It's not that they don't like their prospective daughter- or son-in-law, but they just want to be careful.

Parents can't force an adult child to create a prenup. The only recourse concerned parents have is to carefully plan their own estate, creating trusts that will spring to life after their death and preserve the assets. This is called "the hand from the grave," and the reality is as unpleasant as the image.

So if there's family money involved, don't treat it as a test of your loyalties to either family or your betrothed, pulling you in both directions. This is the perfect center ground on which to make your deal work for you.

And if you're a parent, purchasing this gift for your son or daughter (which we hope you will!), please recognize that the greatest love a parent can have for an adult child is the love that lets go, and allows them to create their own life. In the future, your role will be to support them in their decisions, even when those decisions cause them pain.

ARE YOU READY? WELL, GET GOING!

Here's where the big decisions begin. In building this contract there is recognition of your vulnerability to each other, and a letting down of some defenses. There is an acknowledgment that you two are creating a bigger picture, which sweeps smaller conflicts and disappointments from your path. Ultimately it is best if this process of navigating your contract experience enhances your relationship. But even if conflict arises in the process, the end of a conflict could also be the beginning of a new and better way of relating to each other.

It's said the road to hell is paved with good intentions. There's a reason it's such a common statement—because people lack the energy, self-discipline, or motivation to do what they know in their hearts to be important and true. We are trying to help you pave the way in the other direction—to a heavenly relationship that is built on trust, respect, understanding, and concern for your partner's well-being.

It is our firm belief that this process of navigating your contract will enhance your relationship. In walking this path together, you will reveal your vulnerability to each other, and let down some of your defenses. But you will build the foundation for communication that is so essential to relationship harmony.

This is not all about the art of the deal. It's about the process of creating a balanced, open relationship, now and in the future. It is about opening yourself up to your partner and sharing your fears and vulnerabilities, without worrying that it will give your beloved an edge. After all, what kind of hope do you have of a lasting relationship if you're always playing defense?

Equally, the process of creating this agreement is an opportunity for you to demonstrate your understanding of your partner's concerns and worries. Surely, you don't want to live with someone who is always walking on eggshells to avoid your anger when disagreements arise. That's certainly not a recipe for relationship longevity.

Your Love Deal will require compromise, but that should not be an obstacle. Compromise is the essence of respect and self-respect—as long as one partner does not dominate, nor demand a one-sided solution to all issues. The process of discussion, negotiation, and finding solutions requires openness and integrity. Those are also the requirements of a successful relationship.

Building that relationship starts with the first step you take together to create your New Love Deal. Make it a step in the right direction. We wish you happiness, good health, and a long life together.

We dedicate this book to those we love . . .
and those who find love.

Laws change quickly and new judicial precedents are set frequently at both the state and federal level. Although we will update many of these changes at www.TheNewLoveDeal. com, we urge you to seek your own legal representation and financial counsel, who will advise on appropriate actions for your personal situation.

CPSIA information can be obtained at www.ICGtesting.com
Printed in the USA
LVOW01s2359100215

426473LV00031B/1385/P

9 780615 948089